D1196244

# STAND AND DELIVER

# Stand and Deliver

## The fine art of presentation

Ralph L. Kliem and Irwin S. Ludin

## Gower

Published by
Gower Publishing Limited
Gower House
Croft Road
Aldershot
Hampshire GU11 3HR
England

Gower
Old Post Road
Brookfield
Vermont 05036
USA

British Library Cataloguing in Publication Data
Kliem, Ralph L.
  Stand and Deliver: Fine Art of Presentation
  I. Title II.  Ludin, Irwin S.
  658.452


ISBN 0-566-07574-1


Library of Congress Cataloging-in-Publication Data
Kliem, Ralph L.
  Stand and deliver: the fine art of presentation/Ralph L. Kliem and Irwin S. Ludin.
    p.    cm.
  ISBN 0-566-07574-1
  1. Business presentations.  2. Public speaking.  I. Ludin, Irwin S.
  II. Title
  HF5718.22.K53    1995
  658.4'52--dc20                                              95-1064
                                                               CIP


Typeset in 11pt Goudy by Poole Typesetting (Wessex) Limited and printed in Great Britain by Biddles Ltd, Guildford.

# Dedication

To


Frances Alvidrez – RLK

Leland and Louise Horner – ISL

# Preface

When you have to give a presentation, do you find it hard to:

- Control nervousness?
- Determine what to say?
- Define your audience?
- Organize your content?
- Give your delivery?
- Use visual aids?
- Answer questions?

Even for top-notch presenters the answers don't come easy. In this book Demosthenes – the famous Greek orator – reveals six Pebbles of Wisdom (POWs) to help you prepare and deliver presentations designed to inform, explain and persuade.

Based on these POWs, Demosthenes provides checklists that you can use to create presentations that shine.

Giving a presentation need no longer mean sweaty palms, a pounding heart and knocking knees. *Stand and Deliver* shows you how to prepare and deliver presentations with confidence and in a style which can only lead to personal and professional success.

Ralph L. Kliem
Irwin S. Ludin

# Chapter 1

David Michaels walked aimlessly through the city park. Why do I have to give formal presentations? he thought. Can't I just say I have a really good idea and do my own thing? Why must I give presentations to get what I need?

David shuddered. About the only time he had formally spoken before a group of people was at the victory celebration after moving an entire zoo. And that was a horrifying experience. Now, he was up against greater odds and fears, giving a formal presentation.

Maybe, he thought, I'll learn something about giving presentations by watching other people. He sat on a barren bench facing a small crowd listening to a lonely figure dressed in tattered clothes and waving his arms about his head. Never seen anything like this, he thought. Hope I don't make a fool of myself next week like this guy.

David unfurled a newspaper and read, paying attention partly to the words on the paper and partly to the words of the speaker. As he turned a page he felt a slight rocking of the bench. He peered through the corner of his eye.

What a peculiar looking fellow, he thought. This guy looks like something pulled out of another era. He wore a white frock and sandals. His left cheek bulged as a rubbing sound emerged from between his lips.

'Nice day', said the stranger, spitting out something small.

David lowered the paper away from his face. 'Yeah.' He eased himself further from the man. He then raised the paper and started to read.

'I come here often. And you?' asked the stranger. 'I enjoy watching the pigeons.'

He lowered the paper again. 'No. This is my first time.'

'A visitor, I take it?'

'Yes. Yes, I am', said David. 'Why do you ask?'

'Just curious.' The stranger pointed to the speaker standing before the crowd. 'That pigeon, er, fellow over there. He sure isn't earning his keep. I wonder what he'll get fed? His presentation skills won't earn him any drachmas tonight.'

'I suppose not', said David Michaels. 'I can't judge him as I'm not much of a speaker myself. Can't stand to get in front of a crowd. Scares the living daylights out of me.'

'Not me', said the stranger. 'Not at all. I find it one of the most rewarding parts of life. Nothing like getting in front of a crowd and giving a super presentation. The applause and kudos at the end make it all worthwhile.'

'What are you? An actor?' David asked.

'I guess, in a manner of speaking, I am. But not in the way that you think. Let me introduce myself. The name is Demosthenes.'

'Who? That sounds … '

'Greek.'

'Yeah, Greek', said David, scratching his head. 'Demosthenes? Where did I hear that name before?'

'Here's a clue. King Philip of Macedon was no friend of mine. In fact, a downright enemy.'

2

David couldn't take the clue. Politics was not one of his strengths or assets. 'Sorry, I know very little of Greek politics.'

'Maybe this will help. I am a statesman, orator, lawyer. I speak with rocks in my mouth.' Demosthenes spat a pebble high into the air; the end of its arc hit an empty bottle lying on its side some distance away.

'Not bad. Been practising long?' asked David.

'No, just a few hours a day for over two millennia ... give or take a few generations.'

David froze. He felt chills run up and down his spine as he looked into the dark brown eyes of Demosthenes. It can't be, he thought. 'Are you who ... ?'

'Don't say anything', said Demosthenes. 'Not a thing. Just listen to me. I don't want to perform mouth-to-mouth resuscitation on you. One of my rocks might roll down your throat and choke you. You'll be stoned to death, so to speak.

'I heard your plea for help. Help in giving some formal presentations regarding big improvements on this earth. So, help is here.'

'I need more than a friend. I need a miracle', said David.

Demosthenes rose, took a bow and said: 'At your service.' He then straightened and gestured over to the lonely man speaking before the crowd. 'Please observe the buffoon standing before the audience. This will be your first lesson.'

David looked and watched. He watched as people treated the man with utter disrespect. Some made hissing sounds while others let out boisterous laughs. Several people made obscene gestures while still others tossed peanuts and hard candies.

'Your worst fears?' asked Demosthenes.

'No, not really.' David rubbed his hands through his hair. 'But, they do rank with death and taxes.'

'I see', said Demosthenes, revealing a smirk. He sat and put his arm around David's shoulders. 'Now fill me in on the details.'

'Well, Demosthenes ... '

'My friends call me Demost for short.'

'Well, Demost, I have this proposition for the Yuggenheim Foundation. I want to pursue a project. The biggest project of my life. But it requires capital. Lots of it. And it's a three-step process to getting that capital', continued David. 'First, I must go before a projects council to present my business proposition. The purpose is to inform them of my idea. It's like a summary for executives. Then I go before an executive committee. There I explain in more detail what is required to make the project a reality. Then I must go before a board of directors and persuade them to adopt my business proposition.'

Demost reached into his pocket, removed a pebble, and tossed it into his mouth like popcorn.

'Doesn't that hurt your teeth?' asked David.

'I'll tell you later', snapped Demost. 'Tell me the specifics about your capital idea.'

'It has to do with the Amazon', said David.

'The Amazons?' asked Demosthenes with excitement. 'Female warriors? What interests you in them?'

'Not Amazons', said David. 'Amazon. It's a river in South America. I want to build a healthcare site in the Amazon jungle. A hospital for poor, underprivileged children in the bush. It would include a hospital ship to go up and down the Amazon River to bring sick and dying children back to the base facility, especially for the acute cases. Both the hospital and ship would be entirely self-supporting.'

'Going to become another Jason and the Argonauts?' asked Demosthenes.

'Who's that?' asked David. 'A rock band?'

Demosthenes smiled. 'Definitely not. Jason set sail for the golden fleece. His sailors were called Argonauts because his ship was called Argo. Your proposition reminded me of Jason. Sounds to me it's going to cost you more than one golden fleece. A lot of drachmas to be exact. How do the Yuggenheims feel about that?'

4

'I don't know. My first presentation, the one to the New Projects Council, is next week. If only I can make it to the Board of Directors ... '

'You will, *poulaki mou*', assured Demosthenes.

'*Poulaki mou?*' asked David, not knowing whether to feel insulted or complimented.

'Translated it means little bird in an affectionate sort of way. I see you as a little bird preparing for its first flight', said the Greek. 'I will teach you what you need to know to fly successfully, *poulaki mou*.'

'I just hope', said David with a pounding heart and looking at the speaker, 'that I fly like an eagle, and not like a turkey.'

# Chapter 2

'I'll have red wine with ice', said David, waving his hands to clear the smoke from the air as he spoke to the large waiter who looked more like a bouncer. He had been to nightclubs before but never one this classy. In the centre of the room was an empty stage.

'Nero[1] for me', remarked Demost. 'And Demetri, bring some cheeses and olives.'

Across the room was a band playing folk songs with a harp-like instrument, goatskin bagpipes, and flutes.

'Good music', said David as he surveyed the area. 'Nice place, Demost.'

'Welcome to the Parthenon Tavern. I own it.'

'Really? It figures you'd own a place with a stage.'

'For every presenter, any place is a stage. Tell me, David, what do you know about the communication process?'

'The what?'

'The communication process. What do you know about it?'

---

[1]Nero: a mineral water.

'Nothing really, I guess', said David as he took his glass of wine from the waiter. 'Why?'

'Looks like I'm going to have to turn this experience into a beginners' class', said Demost, and sighed deeply. 'The communication process is simple, really. It involves two main players. Know who they are?'

David took a sip from his drink and went into deep thought. 'Let me guess, here … I … think it's the presenter … '

'Right. And … '

'The audience.'

'You got it', said Demost. He spat a small pebble into his drink and then sipped his mineral water. 'Both play an integral role in the communication process.' He removed a pen from his pocket and drew something on a napkin. 'Look at this.'

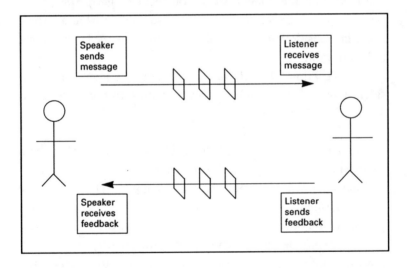

'See those boxes in the middle? They're nothing more than a set of filters that words pass through. Each set consists of values, beliefs, norms, you name it. Each listener has a different set of filters', continued Demost. 'A presenter must recognize that his words travel through these filters. And some filters are thicker than others. By the time the message reaches the listener, some aspects of the message don't make it or they're altered. All because of those filters.'

'Yeah, but what about the presenter?' asked David.

'The presenter receives feedback from the listener.'

'And', added David, 'the feedback goes through filters.'

'I say, you are indeed a quick student.' Demost took a sip from his drink. 'So what can happen if a speaker ignores this simple but profound description of the communication process?'

David took a gulp from his drink, only this time keeping some crushed ice in his mouth as he spoke. 'The presenter needs to be aware of these filters; otherwise the message may be interpreted the wrong way. Or', continued David, 'the presenter may ignore the feedback, incorrectly responding to the listener.'

'Good. Tell me, David, since you seem to grasp the fundamentals of the communication process so quickly, what are some essential considerations for analysing your audience before giving a presentation?'

'I don't know.' David rubbed his chin. 'I guess one consideration is what commonalities you share with the audience ... and ... the differences.'

'Good. And what else?'

'Their needs, desires and beliefs.' David fidgeted in his chair. 'Also who are the people in the audience ... '

'Especially the key ones', Demost quipped. 'Here are three other considerations. You should determine who disagrees with you, why, and develop ways to learn from those disagreements.

'You can also determine who agrees with you, why, and develop ways to reinforce those agreements. And you can ascertain the audience's knowledge, expertise and interest level on the subject you are discussing. Keeping the communication process in mind, let's discuss the three basic types of presentation.'

'Sounds good to me', said David. 'What are they?'

'Ah, the impatience of youth.'

'I'm thirty years old', said David.

'Compared to a man almost twenty-five hundred years old, you're a youth.'

'Good point', David said, straightening himself in his chair.

'Now I'll use analogy for the first type of presentation. Just like the way Socrates used to teach. If I tell you what happened during the Peloponnesian War, what type of presentation would I be giving?'

'The Pelo ... what?'

'The Peloponnesian War. The war mainly between Athens and Sparta.'

'Oh', said David. 'Well, I say you'd be giving an informative presentation. Just like my presentation before the New Projects Council.'

'Good', said Demosthenes. 'Now if I told you how Sparta crushed my beloved Athens, what type of presentation would that be?'

'Let's see', said David, as he rubbed his chin. 'I'd say it's a presentation to explain.'

'An explanatory presentation, to be exact.'

'Just like the one I'll give before the Executive Steering Committee.'

'Very good', said Demosthenes.

'Now if I tried to convince you that Alcibiades was not a bad general or lacked moral scruples that ... '

'Wait a second', said David, raising his hand. 'Alcibi who?'

'Alcibiades. He was an Athenian military and political leader who led Athens into war against Sparta. He committed infidelities. Cut lucrative deals with the Spartans.'

'So', said David, 'the guy cheated on his wife, lost a war, and took money from the enemy and you want to try to convince me he wasn't a bad general or lacked moral scruples?'

'Yes', said Demosthenes with a smile.

'That's going to take some persuasion.' Then a light turned on in his head. 'Persuasion. A persuasive presentation. That's the third type of presentation. Just like I'll have to give before the Board of Directors.'

'Excellent.'

'Wow', David said. 'I never thought there was so much to giving good presentations. Tell me more.'

'There is more. Lots more. But you're far from ready for the big boys' stuff.'

'But Demost ... '

'Sorry. Besides, it's getting late. It's clean-up time for the club and I'm growing tired.'

'But Demost', persisted David, 'I'm learning some good stuff here.'

'I understand, David. But when you get over two thousand years old you grow tired early. Time for bed. I'll call you, don't you call me.' Demost then pointed at a waiter standing in a distant dark corner. It was Demetri.

'I ... ' By the time David looked back across the table at his new friend Demost was gone. And before Demetri could take one step further David was gone, too.

# Chapter 3

Physically and mentally tired, David removed the key to his rented apartment. As he turned the key, he felt an abrupt pull on the door.

The door swung open. There stood a short, pudgy, grey-haired woman. A wide grin was painted across her face as she raised her arms to embrace him. 'Ah, my handsome son!'

'Hi, mom', he said. He hugged her and worked his way to the couch in the living room. He plopped on to it.

'Where have you been? You smell of cigarette smoke and alcohol. You don't do this every night, do you?' She sat next to him. 'You look so down. Who is she, son?'

'Mom, it's no one. I ... '

'Oh my poor child, what's wrong?'

'Nothing, mom, nothing. I just met this guy. He's Greek ... '

'He's what?'

'Greek, mom.'

'Greek? How long have you known him?'

'I just met him tonight.'

'Was he bearing gifts ... ?'

'Look mom, don't turn your visit into a non-stop torture session. I've got enough pressure on me right now.'

'What is it? You can tell your mom everything.'

'Well, okay.' He raised himself on the couch and looked directly at her. 'You promise not to get excited?'

She nodded her head.

'Good.' He eased over to her and kissed her on the forehead. 'You're a good mom. The best.'

A warm smile illuminated her face. 'You're a good son. What's bothering you?'

'I'm between jobs.'

'Oh my God!' She rose from the couch. 'I don't understand. You had a good job. You had a good education. Your father, rest his soul, worked hard for you to have a better life … '

'Mom, you promised not to get excited. You … ' He stood up with his arms reaching out for her. 'Now mom, you promised … '

She calmed down and sat on the easy chair across from the couch. He sat opposite her.

'No, mom, let me explain. I'm not a kid anymore. I'm thirty years old … '

'Not married yet either. Where are my grandchildren? Your brother Tommy already gave me two.' Tears started to form in her eyes.

'Mom, let's drop that, can we? You want to hear what I want to tell you or not?'

She nodded her head and mumbled 'Okay.'

'I quit my job at the Yuggenheim Foundation to pursue something that's special to me. I can't do it as a regular employee because those monies have been committed for the next five years', he explained. He took a deep breath and continued. 'But they do set aside funds for special projects that provide a public service. This money can only be allocated to special projects. And once started the Foundation has absolutely no control over them. In return for their philanthropy they get additional tax write-offs and worldwide recognition. Basically, it meant quitting my job and doing what I want to do.'

'And what's that?' asked his mother with a bewildered look on her face.

'The special project? Well, what I want to do is set up a complete self-supporting healthcare facility in the Amazon jungle to help sick and dying children. There would be a hospital site and also a hospital ship to go up and down the Amazon River and its tributaries. The whole set-up, including the ship, would be essentially a self-supporting colony ... '

'I'm so proud of you, son. It's a noble thought but don't you think you're in for a disappointment? Don't you have to sell this idea to somebody?'

'Yeah, eventually to the Board of Directors.'

She rose from her chair and walked over to sit next to her son. 'I don't understand your work, son. But keep talking. Get it out of your system. You'll feel better.'

'It means I have to go before the Board of Directors to get my wish. I not only have to inform them and explain my mission but I must go one step further.'

'Yes, my darling son?'

'I must persuade them through a presentation to approve my business proposition. Otherwise, more children could suffer, even die.'

A long silence ensued.

'Son?'

'Yes, mom?'

'I love you, you know that. So don't take what I say personally, will you?'

He felt suddenly wide awake, knowing that his mother was setting the stage for delivering criticism, something she could do very well at times.

'Son, you need to work on your appearance. You really do. Look at you. Your tie is crooked. You need a haircut. Your suit is always ruffled. And your shoes need polishing. Besides, you've always been awkward in front of an audience. Remember in your high school play how everybody made fun of you? And you only had three lines. It almost drove you to a nervous breakdown. Don't do this to yourself. Son, you're not the salesman type', she said. She took a deep sigh and continued. 'I think you should be doing something else, like holding down a steady job. Maybe even getting married and having children.'

'Mom, don't start!' He rose from the couch and headed for the bedroom. 'I'm tired.'

'Son, you didn't tell me about this Greek boy you met.'

He turned round as he walked towards the bedroom door. 'Mom, he's a famous, experienced speaker. That's all. He owns a nightclub and he's older than you', snapped David. He then turned and headed again to the bedroom.

'Well, maybe he can teach you something about speaking in front of an audience so you don't make a fool of yourself.'

'Good night!' he said as he slammed the bedroom door behind him.

# Chapter 4

Stepping into the entrance of the nightclub felt like a step into another world. Outside, the sounds, people and machines shook David's eardrums. Inside, he felt a quietude, even a sense of serenity. He looked around, noticing nobody was present. Not even the owner, Demosthenes.

'Demost', he said lightly.

Nothing.

'Demost, are you here?'

Still nothing.

Strange, he thought. The place was left open and unattended.

'Explain to me the communication process', ordered a voice from the dark stage in the centre of the lounge.

'The communication process?' David asked in a low voice. 'It contains filters that let some information pass through and some not.'

'Precisely. You do learn quickly', said Demosthenes. 'The communication process is really part of the six POWs of giving effective presentations.' The lights over the stage came on, revealing the Greek.

'What?' asked David. 'The six POWs?' He walked over to a table and sat facing the stage.

Demosthenes marched off the stage and approached the table. 'The six POWs or Pebbles of Wisdom. By mastering the six POWs, you will be able to conquer the fear of getting in front of an audience, whatever type of presentation that you give. You've learned the essence of the first one.'

'I have?'

'Perspective', said Demosthenes as he sat at the table. 'Perspective.'

'That means knowing your audience and yourself so you'll have the ability to see things from certain vantage points.' David sought verification. 'Correct?'

'Correct', replied Demosthenes. 'But you need to remember just a little bit more about perspective.'

'Really?'

Demosthenes rose from the table and walked over to a set of switches on the wall. He dimmed the lights until it was almost pitch black.

David watched the Greek's silhouette move towards a second wall panel and toy with another set of switches. The room grew cooler as he heard what he assumed to be Demosthenes' footsteps approaching his table.

'Feeling a bit different?' asked Demosthenes.

'Yeah, so?' David tried to sound confident but he felt himself grow nervous. He wanted to rise and leave, worried that maybe the old man was crazy and ready to do something weird. But he remembered the words of his mother last night when she said he might learn something from the ancient Greek.

'Well?' asked Demosthenes. 'What are the other nuances of perspective?' David felt nervous as the walls of the lounge suddenly seemed to close in on him and the silence suffocate him.

Demosthenes started a disquisition on the history and philosophy of ancient Greece.

But David did not listen. The coolness and darkness affected his attention span.

Suddenly the Greek stopped speaking. The silence lasted for several minutes but seemed longer. David shuffled in his chair and tapped the top of the table. The sounds of his pounding fingertips echoed throughout the lounge.

'Demosthenes? Speak to me, will you?' David pushed the chair back and started to rise.

'Stay seated', commanded Demosthenes. 'I'm proving a point.'

David slid back into his chair. 'And what's that?'

'You just witnessed it.'

David heard the Greek push back his chair and walk away.

'Where are you going, Demost?' asked David.

No comment. He watched the Greek's silhouette move towards the air conditioning switches and then to the light switches. Demosthenes then returned to the table.

David felt the room becoming warmer and he felt more comfortable. 'Well, that was different', he said with a sigh.

'Good.' Demosthenes leaned forward on the table. 'You feel different now?'

'You bet.' David relaxed in his chair. 'What did you do that for?'

Demosthenes smiled. 'How did you feel when the room was dark and cooler?'

'Nervous. I was ready to leave.'

'Can you repeat to me what I said about the history and philosophy of my beautiful Greece?'

'Not a word', said David, apologetically.

'Precisely my point.' Demosthenes leaned over the table. 'Perspective is also influenced by environment. The environment the audience finds itself in. If I told you the same thing now, you would be more receptive, would you not?'

David nodded.

'It is important, *poulaki mou*, to research your environment before giving a presentation because it will affect how people receive your message. Can you list some other factors?'

17

David felt an answer pop from his brain to his tongue. 'Factors about the location where the presentation will be given.'

'Right. Why?'

'If the room is too small, stuffy or dark the audience may not focus on what you have to say.'

'Now, give me another factor.'

David rubbed his chin as he thought. 'I know – how many people will be there.'

'Right again. Why?'

'The number of people influences how you present the material. Too many may inhibit people's receptivity to what you have to say. Especially if interaction is necessary.' David felt more confident.

'Give me another environmental condition.'

'When the meeting occurs.'

'Perfect', said Demosthenes. 'Why?'

'The time of day and the length of the presentation can influence how well they perceive and receive your message', answered David.

'When's a definite bad time to give a presentation?'

'I bet late afternoons, like four-thirty, is a bad time.'

Demosthenes looked at his watch. 'Good point. I'll be ... it's four-thirty now. We'll talk another time. The lounge opens in half an hour. And like this watch, I've got to get things ticking. There's work to do. The band will be arriving to set up their instruments and the dancers will soon be here, too. The cook must prepare *dolmathes*,[1] *souvlaki*,[2] *moussaka*,[3] *pastitsio*[4] and salads.'

'But you said there are six POWs to learn', persisted David.

---

[1]*Dolmathes*: stuffed grape leaves with eggs and lemon sauce.
[2]*Souvlaki*: grilled lamb.
[3]*Moussaka*: aubergine and minced meat.
[4]*Pastitsio*: meat and macaroni.

'There really are more. I just made up a seventh one', Demosthenes said with a chuckle.

'What's that?'

'Patience. And that's something I'm running out of if we don't end this conversation now.' The Greek's smile disappeared. 'You do see my viewpoint?'

'Sure, Demost', said David, rising and heading towards the exit. 'But it's not mine.'

# Chapter 5

David said nothing while sitting at the dinner table. His nostrils inhaled the aroma of his mother's homemade spaghetti.

'What's the matter, son? Something wrong?' she asked.

'No', he said, shaking his head from side to side. 'Nothing.'

'Then eat. You'll get skinny.'

'Mom, I'm not that hungry.' He picked up his fork but dropped it back on the table. 'I can't eat.'

'You'll get sick. It's that presentation, isn't it?'

He looked her straight in the eyes. 'Yeah.'

'What's bothering you? You can certainly tell your mother, can't you?'

David balked at responding. He remained quiet. He did not want to upset her, let alone get into an argument.

'Did that Greek tell you something? Is that what's bothering you?' She rose from her chair and walked over to where he sat. She wrapped her arms around his shoulders and gave him a hug and a kiss on the forehead. Then she sat back down into her chair.

'Mom, it's not Demosthenes ... '

'Then what?'

The urge to unload on his mother was too strong. 'I just don't know', he said. 'I just don't know … '

'Know what? Tell me while you eat.'

'Mom, I don't think I can go forward with my business proposition. I've got three days to give the first presentation and I'm not ready.'

'Why? It means so much to you.'

'I know. But I hate giving presentations. And I'm not good at it. I'm a manager, not a presenter. I should never have quit my job.'

'I told you', she said, pointing her finger at him. 'You had a good job. But … '

'But what?'

'But, that's in the past. You are a Michaels! You can't quit now! Your father, rest his soul, never quit at anything.'

The word 'quitting' made his stomach churn. The look of spicy, garlic-laced spaghetti sauce didn't make his guts feel any better either. Still, he did not want to hurt his mother's feelings. He forced forkfuls of white noodles dressed in red down his throat.

'You're a good boy. You'll make some lucky girl a good husband. If I should live so long.'

'Don't start, mom.'

'I'm not starting anything. It's you. Look at yourself. Sitting there like a whipped pup', she continued. 'Your father … '

'Don't bring dad into this', he warned as he slapped his hand on the table.

'Son, I'm just trying to prove a point.'

David said with a growl: 'What point is that?'

'You have to be more self-confident. Be stronger, just like your father. He was such a brave man. A good man, rest his soul. He was a great showman. One of the best.'

'Dad made presentations?' David never knew much about his father. He died when David was eight years old.

'Your father was a very expressive man but still pleasant to be around', she said. She released a big sigh then continued. 'He was a real dynamo. I remember when he ran for public office.'

'Dad ran for office?'

'Oh yes, for mayor. But he lost because of political corruption at the polls. Yes dear, your father was quite the showman.'

'Didn't he ever get nervous?'

'Oh yes', she said in a soft voice. 'Of course. He would always tell me that minutes before giving a presentation he would get these terrible butterflies in his stomach.' She rubbed her stomach in imitation. 'But he would stand before his audience with great poise because he was well organized, knew a lot about his subject, and talked naturally. But ... ' She waved her hands in front of her face and grimaced, ' ... but sometimes after he finished, he would sweat so badly from being nervous that his clothes would be soaking wet. He'd always bring a change of clothes just in case this happened. It really wasn't his fault but it was pretty gruesome. His soul should rest in peace.'

'I didn't know that Dad could speak in front of an audience', said David in a surprised tone, but he felt a strong sense of confidence and pride. 'And was he nervous?'

'Very. He was such a baby in many ways.'

David rose from his chair and walked over to his mother and gave her a big hug. 'You're the best mom in the whole world.'

The phone rang. His mother picked up the handset. 'Hello ... Yes ... He's right here. May I ask who's calling? Demosthenes? Are you that ... '

David snatched the handset from her. 'Demost?'

'Why don't you come over to the lounge?' asked Demosthenes. 'We can play a game of chess. You do play chess?'

'I'll be right over.'

# Chapter 6

David entered through the front door of the lounge. A huge, heavy-set man greeted him. It was Demetri.

'You Mr Michaels?' Demetri asked.

'Yeah', said David. He felt minuscule as the man stepped closer.

'Da boss is waiting for ya', said the man as he led the way to a room behind the stage. David noticed that the stage was empty even though a dozen or so people sat around drinking. 'Boss. Mr Michaels is here.'

'Let him in', said Demosthenes. He laid a book next to the marble chess set resting on his table.

The two men exchanged pleasantries and then positioned themselves to play the game.

Demosthenes made the first move as they talked.

'So, now you know the first POW of giving effective presentations. And that is?'

'Perspective ... ' said David as he thought about his next move.

'Is your perspective ready for the next POW?'

'Sure, what is it?'

'Not so fast', said Demost as he took another of David's pawns.

'I'll give you a clue. It's to do with how people perceive you, not only how you perceive them.'

'Me?'

'That's right. To a large extent, it has to do with how you manage your own nervous energy and even the nervous energy from the audience.'

'What do you mean?' asked David.

'It's how you project yourself. How you convey confidence.'

'Oh I see', said David. The discussion he had earlier with his mother came to mind. 'You mean the way I seem to the audience.'

'Right.' The Greek speaker spat a pebble squarely into the spittoon next to the table and then moved his rook.

'Let me guess what some of those perceptions are', David said with excitement. 'A presenter has to be clear yet enthusiastic, even expressive to a certain degree.'

'Very good … '

David moved a pawn forward. 'He must be pleasant but not docile. He must be organized but sensitive to the needs and emotions of the audience while at the same time appearing natural.'

'Excellent, David. Any more?'

'He needs to show that he has an understanding and knowledge of the subject matter. Good poise and self-esteem should be there as well.'

'Why David, how did you learn all this?'

'My mom and I talked about how I appear to people.'

'Well', said Demosthenes. 'Mother does know best. A very perceptive woman.' He directed his attention from the chess board and peered at David. 'Perhaps we should meet some day.' Demosthenes' knight then seized David's queen. 'So she taught you the second POW?'

The answer shot him right between the ears. 'Perception.'

'Excellent', said Demosthenes. 'Now it's time to learn what the next POW stands for.'

'Can't wait', said David. He moved his knight.

'I'll take that.' Demost snatched up the chess piece and replaced it with his rook.

'How did you do that?' David prided himself on his own chess-playing ability; never had he seen better playing.

'It doesn't just happen', said Demosthenes with a sigh. He looked up at David. 'It takes solid strategy and top tactics. Just like a presentation.'

'A presentation?' David failed to see the similarities.

'Yes', said Demosthenes. 'Your move.'

David thought for a while and then made his move. 'Good stuff.'

'Well, as I was saying, as in chess, you need a good strategy when giving a presentation. You know what that means, don't you?'

'Let's see', said David, rubbing his chin and looking down at the chess board. 'It means knowing what you want to accomplish in your presentation.'

'Good', said Demost. 'But there's something else.' He made the next move. 'Your turn.'

David moved his bishop four squares. 'I think I know. Let's see … yeah … structuring your presentation helps you achieve your goals.'

'Keeping in mind what is meant by strategy, you should be able to give me a good definition of tactics.'

'How's this?' David proudly moved his bishop two squares to directly threaten Demost's king. 'I guess tactics are really the actions or manoeuvres a presenter takes in executing his strategy.' David looked up with a smile. 'Check!'

The Greek fell back into his chair. 'Hmmm … Tactics allow you to do three things. One is to strengthen the main ideas of the presentation … '

'Another', added David, 'is to build bridges to join those ideas.'

'Right', said Demosthenes. 'But there is just one more. Good tactics add credibility and reputability to the presenter.'

Demosthenes manoeuvred his bishop to protect his king while taking David's bishop. 'And that's exactly what you lack right here.'

Two moves later Demosthenes spoke. 'Checkmate!'

David stared at the board. He was unable to utter even a sound. It was a brilliant move.

'Care for something to drink while we have another game?' asked Demosthenes. 'Or are you done for the evening?'

# Chapter 7

David soothed his nerves with a cup of coffee. 'Now it's my turn.' He set down the cup and rubbed his hands together before taking up a knight and making the next move.

'Hmmm, let's see.' Demost kept his focus on the table as he continued. 'The strategy and tactics you employ in a presentation depend heavily on the type of presentation you give.'

'The type of presentation?' asked David.

'That's right.' Demost moved his queen. 'You may remember, there are three types. Want to venture to guess them again?' He spat a pebble.

David tapped his fingers on the table as he talked and concentrated at the same time. 'I know there's the kind to just convey information to people.' He made a move.

'That's right', said the Greek as he made the next move. 'The idea is to communicate information. That's all.'

'I guess it would be like a presentation on corporate earnings for a fiscal quarter or how a disease has affected a given population. Or like my first presentation before the New Projects Council. An *informative* presentation.'

'I think you've got it memorized, by Zeus.'

A long silence ensued as David focused on his next move. 'You want me to guess the next type of presentation?'

'I'll ask the questions on giving presentations, if you don't mind', said Demost. 'But just to satisfy your immense craving for knowledge I'll tell you. After you make your move. We don't have all night.'

'Okay', said David, sheepishly. He moved his rook.

'The next type of presentation is called an *explanatory* presentation. 'Can you tell me what that means?'

'It builds on the informative presentation by providing an understanding of how something works.' David made his next move.

'Can you give me an example?'

David thought for a minute. 'Yeah. How I got to this point in the chess game.'

'That would be one. Any others?'

'My second presentation, before the Executive Steering Committee, is another.'

Demost nodded. 'That's right. In what way?'

'Well ... I will explain how I got the idea, why the New Projects Council agreed with me, and explain how I would deploy it and ... '

'That's enough. You've got the idea.' Demost made the next move. 'That leaves the third type. What is it?'

'Demost, you're not too convincing.'

'Want to bet?' asked Demost, making his next move. 'You just used a related word.'

'A related word to convincing?' asked David. He moved his bishop across the board and smiled. 'I know the word. It's persuade.' David looked at the Greek, noticing the man's hands running through his grey hair. 'Check.'

'I see that you do catch on very quickly. What's the goal of a *persuasive* presentation?' Demost positioned a bishop to protect his king.

'To convince the audience of your way of thinking or opinion. Just like my final presentation before the Board of Directors.' David lifted his eyes from the chess table and looked directly at Demost. 'Checkmate!'

Demost coughed as his eyes raced across the board. He motioned several times to make his move but found nothing. He then fell back into his chair. 'Yes, indeed, David. You do learn very quickly.'

'And by the way', added David, as he picked up the cup of coffee and raised it in the air, 'the third POW stands for planning.'

# Chapter 8

The evening sun worked its way behind the huge spruce and oak trees which stood in the distance. I don't want to go home again, thought David. Mom would just hassle me and besides, the impending presentation is terrifying me.

He opted for a walk in the park. It was the same park where he had met Demost. Only this time he would listen to the cast of characters scattered throughout the park giving speeches and presentations covering everything from drug trafficking sanctioned by the government to the rights of the tsetse fly.

David planted his bottom on a bench, not too far from a young man dressed in a pair of torn jeans and an orange sweatshirt. He watched and listened as the man spoke before a dozen or so people. David struggled to hear what the man said. All he could tell was that it had something to do with destroying the jungles of Central America.

'That fellow stinks as a speaker', said a voice from behind him.

David turned. 'What ... ?'

'I thought I'd join you here at the park', said the Greek as he sat himself next to his young student. 'I don't want you to think that I'm a bad loser.'

'Well, you can't win at everything', said David.

'Lost a few speech contests in the past', said Demosthenes. 'But won more than I lost. Besides … '

'Besides what?' asked David, directing his attention towards the speaker.

'I let you win.'

David turned his attention back to the Greek. 'You didn't!'

'You do get startled fast, don't you?' The Greek pointed to the man speaking. 'Now there's a real loser. Let's turn this into a review. What do you think of him?'

For several minutes David sat, observed and took mental notes.

'Well?' Demosthenes asked.

'Can hardly hear him. Doesn't pronounce words very well', observed David. 'He just rambles.'

'His joints seem stiffer than mine and I'm over two thousand years older', said Demost, reaching down to the ground, lifting a pebble and popping it in his mouth. 'The man has a bad case of rigor mortis.'

'Yeah', agreed David. 'He's not very dynamic or doesn't have, you know … ' He struggled with the word.

'Poise', said Demosthenes. 'Poise.'

'Yeah, that's it. Poise', said David, snapping his fingers. 'I guess the people listening to him have nothing better to do at this time of night.'

'I do', snapped Demost. 'I think it's time to watch another speaker', he said as he rose from the bench. 'Follow me.'

David did, to another bench several metres away.

'Now that lad has potential', said Demosthenes. 'He exudes confidence and enthusiasm. And look at the way he moves around!'

31

No doubt about it, thought David, the delivery was not bad. But there was something about the speech that perplexed him.

'What a motor mouth', said Demost. 'This fellow rambles, too. A bad case of logorrhoea. Shut his beak!' He covered his ears in a mocking gesture. He then removed his hands. 'In case you don't know, logorrhoea is, colloquially speaking, diarrhoea of the mouth. Now, why do you think that's so?'

'Ah ... ', said David, struggling to pull out an answer. Then it came. 'There's no strategy to his presentation.'

'Good boy. What else?'

'Can't tell what type of presentation. Informative? Explanatory? Persuasive?'

'He might as well speak to Turks', said Demosthenes. 'What we need to observe is someone who can face the crowd and give a presentation that would cause the walls of the Parthenon to crumble, by Zeus!'

'Who might that be?' asked David.

Demosthenes climbed up on to the bench. He shouted, 'Ladies and gentlemen!'

'What are you doing, Demost?'

'I have before you a man who can fill your ears with the music of the tongue!'

'Who's that?' David asked.

Demosthenes pointed at him.

David watched with fear as a dozen or so onlookers drifted in his direction. Before he could blink his eyes, they surrounded him.

He felt Demost's hand reach down, take hold of his and pull him to his feet. 'This young man wants to help the poor children of the Amazon!'

David's eyes widened as he felt the blood rush through his veins. A sensation, a tingling one, filled his stomach. His palms began to sweat. His breathing quickened. 'Hello ... ', he forced out in a weak voice from a dry mouth while motioning a gentle wave to the onlookers.

'They want you to say more than that', said Demosthenes. He clenched his fist and twirled it in front of the audience and repeatedly shouted, 'More!'

Soon the audience joined Demosthenes' pleas.

'More! More!' they cried.

David seemed paralysed. He could not force any sound from his mouth as he tried to avoid looking into the crowd by gazing over their heads at distant trees and birds. Fear captured his body.

'What a waste', shouted a voice from the crowd.

'He's a clown', agreed another.

'Mommy', said a child, pointing at David. 'Is there something wrong with that man?'

Several people turned to walk away.

'Wait!' commanded David. 'Wait ... '

Some people stopped and turned.

'The Amazon is the ... ah ... mightiest river in the world', shouted David. He took a deep sigh and continued. 'It cuts through ... a lush, green jungle in South America ... and empties its booty into ... the Atlantic Ocean.'

He noticed the people starting to come closer as Demosthenes moved a few feet away.

'Despite this natural beauty there is horror that no human being can ignore.' David felt like he was harnessing the nervousness that consumed him and directed it into his presentation. He became consumed with a self-confidence that he had never before felt. 'Death by disease. And that's the fate that awaits thousands of children each year.'

One woman shook her head in sorrow.

'Many children suffer beyond anyone's imagination', he said. 'I want to help them by building a medical facility and a hospital ship. In a few days, I will present my proposition to the Yuggenheim Foundation.'

Demosthenes rose and lifted his hands into the air. 'That is all, my good friends. That's all. Have a good evening.'

'But, Demost ... '

The Greek put his finger to his lips as a signal to keep quiet.

'But I have more to say, Demost.'

'No you don't!' Demost waved the audience off.

As the last person left David asked, 'Why did you stop me? I was just getting warmed up.'

'Because I only wanted you to feel comfortable in front of an audience', said Demost, 'not give them a lecture on your business proposition. Besides, I cut it short for a reason.'

'Why?'

'I wanted you to get a feel for the importance of perspective, perception and planning. You see, by not employing those three POWs you look and feel very jittery. You then tend to ramble on and on like you started to do. But by using them your confidence increases and your performance gets better.'

'Makes sense', agreed David. 'Well, what do you think?'

'About your performance?' Demost stroked his face. 'Much better than I expected. That's because you knew something about perspective, perception, and planning. What do you think?'

'Yeah, but I was nervous as hell', said David, with a nervous laugh. 'I felt as if I was facing monsters!'

'That's natural', said Demost. 'It's not uncommon to feel as if you're riding on the shoulders of a minotaur.'

'A what?' asked David.

'Minotaur. Half-human, half-bull. After you start feeling more relaxed, you feel you're riding Pegasus, a winged horse.'

Demost took David by the hand and led him from the bench. 'You did something that all presenters must do eventually. And you did it all by yourself. It is the only way.'

'What's that?' asked David.

'Control their nervousness by funnelling that energy into their presentations.'

'Do you get nervous, Demost?'

'Always. As you get older, you get better at controlling it.'

'Even after twenty-five hundred years?'
'I'm going home', said Demost. 'You're making me nervous.'

# Chapter 9

'Mom!' shouted David as he kicked open the door to the apartment. Cradled in one arm was a bag of take-away Chinese food. In the other he held by the neck a bottle of champagne. 'Mom! Come here and help me.'

'What? What is it?' she said, scurrying to the door. She took the bag and carried it away as he locked the door.

'I thought I'd bring home some Chinese food', he said. A proud smile painted his face. 'We have cause for celebration.'

'What?' she asked as she disappeared into another room.

'Tonight, something very special happened.'

'Oh?'

He could hear her setting the table. 'I did it.'

'You're getting married!' she said, coming back into the room. 'I'm going to be a grandmom!'

'No, mom.' He watched a disappointed look come over her face.

He walked across and gave her a big hug. 'No, mom. I'm not getting married.'

'Then what?' she asked as she returned to the other room.

'I gave a sort of presentation tonight', he said proudly as he followed her.

'Sort of? To whom?'

'To a bunch of people in the park. I told them about my business proposition.' He opened the bottle of champagne, which released a loud pop. 'And they loved it.'

'Whose idea was this?'

'Demosthenes'.' He poured the champagne into some glasses. 'You would have been proud of me. You really would. At first, I was scared out of my wits. My body felt as if it had the 'flu. I tell you, if Demost hadn't been there, I would have ... '

'Made a fool of yourself?'

'Yeah', he said. 'But I didn't. Even Demost said I did a good job. You would have been proud of me. Dad would have been proud. I was great. And you know what, mom? I loved it. Really loved it. I now have this sense of confidence about getting in front of a group.'

'There's much more to learn, son. Much more.'

'Demost will teach me. I know he will.'

'But in the end, only you will be in front of the audience. Not Demosthenes. Next time, you could be there all by yourself.'

'Mom, don't give me a lecture. I did well. I really did!'

'What have you learned so far?' she asked.

David took a deep breath and said proudly, 'Three of the six POWs of effective presentations.'

'What's a POW?'

'Pebble of Wisdom.'

'Are these pebbles worth anything?'

'You bet they're worth something. They're worth a lot of somethings. The first POW stands for perspective.'

'That means what?'

'Knowing the audience and yourself so you'll have the ability to see things from different vantage points', he said.

'And what, son, does the second POW stand for?'

'Perception. It deals with how you perceive the audience and how it perceives you.'

'And the third POW?'

'Planning!' David walked back and forth in front of the table. 'It deals with determining in advance the type of presentation you're going to give.' He stopped and pointed his finger into the air. 'Then you can determine the strategy of the presentation and choose the right tactics.' He took a deep breath and felt his chest expand with pride.

'Well, as I said, you still have much to learn.'

'Like what?'

'Like not serving champagne with Chinese food', she said as she turned her head from the champagne. 'Good gracious, didn't I raise you better?'

# Chapter 10

David tossed and turned in his bed as he thought of his presentation before the New Projects Council. The excitement was too much for him to bear. He rose from the bed, put on his plaid bathrobe and headed towards the living room. He picked up the remote control for the colour television and pressed the power button.

Nothing good on, he thought, looking up at the clock on the wall. It was two o'clock in the morning. Nothing good could possibly be on.

But wait. He changed the channel to the public television station. David watched a documentary on great speakers of history.

He listened as the announcer talked about how they moved crowds. How they took facts and organized them in such a way as to encourage people to action. Wow, he thought, I wish I could do that.

There were the famous and the infamous of modern times. Winston Churchill. Abraham Lincoln. Martin Luther King, Jr.

Adolf Hitler. Then the show switched back to antiquity. The narrator talked about a host of unrecognized names.

Except for one.

There before him, on the screen, was a statue of a man with his arm stretched out. David looked closely. There was no doubt about it. The resemblance was uncanny.

Demosthenes.

David increased the volume.

'To many', said the narrator, 'the greatest speaker of ancient Greece was Demosthenes.'

David increased the volume again.

'Born in 384 BC of wealthy parents, he soon lost the privileged status that wealth bestowed upon members of his class. His father died when Demosthenes was just seven. All the wealth was placed in the hands of guardians who squandered it.

'For a long time, Demosthenes failed at public speaking, unable to inspire the Athenian assembly. Of course, his stammering didn't help matters. But Demosthenes was no quitter. He practised untiringly even to the point of doing so with pebbles in his mouth.

'Demosthenes' claim to fame was delivering a series of speeches called the Philippics in an effort to stop the conquests of Alexander the Great's father, Philip II of Macedon. Demosthenes gave three Philippics.

'In the latter part of his life, Demosthenes faced tragic circumstances. He was surrounded by scandal, forced into exile and, although no proof exists, he was rumoured to have killed himself by poison rather than surrender himself to the Macedonians.'

'Wow!' mumbled David. 'I didn't know … '

'Demosthenes' speeches', continued the announcer, 'were always passionate. They rarely struck a humorous note. Instead, they were often filled with sarcasm, even invective. His speeches were clearly structured, arranged logically and filled with examples that could persuade the bitterest opponent. More often than not, his speeches were masterpieces of *logos* and *ethos*, peppered with *pathos*.

'In Rome, the number of fine speakers increased tenfold with men like Cicero ... '

David's eyelids grew tired. '*Ethos. Logos. Pathos.* What are those?' he asked himself as he turned off the television and went to bed.

# Chapter 11

The phone ringing on his bedside table shattered David's peaceful sleep.

'What the ... ?' He rolled over and picked up the receiver. 'Hello.'

'David. It is I.'

'Who?' He could hear music over the receiver.

'I, that's who. Demost. Who else would be listening to *demotiki*[1] in the morning?'

'Demost.' He yawned. 'Guess what?'

'What?'

'I heard about you on television. You're supposed to be dead.'

There was a long silence.

'Did you hear me?' continued David.

'Look', said Demost. 'I didn't call to justify my existence to you. I called because I think you've now reached a stage when you can take a big step forward.'

'I can?'

---

[1]*Demotiki*: Greek folk music.

'I'll ask the questions, if you don't mind. Now', continued Demosthenes, 'I want you to do something.'

David tried to gain full consciousness as he wiped the sleep from his eyes. 'What, Demost?'

'I want you to prepare for me a draft of your first presentation before the New Projects Council.'

'A what?'

'A draft. You know, a handout. I want you to prepare it just the way you would for the New Projects Council.'

'But ... '

'No buts', said Demost. 'I think that would be the right follow-up to the good start you had at the park.'

'I'll need to practise', said David.

'That will follow. But for now I want you to prepare the presentation and give it to me to review.'

'Where?' The adrenaline flowed as if he had already drunk his morning coffee.

'At the lounge. It has everything. I'll keep it closed just for you, *poulaki mou*, so that we can discuss your presentation. I'll see you tonight at eight. Until then ... '

Before David could utter a word, he heard a click and the all too familiar buzzing sound on the receiver.

# Chapter 12

David scratched his head with a pencil as he struggled to build his presentation. Let's see, he thought. How do I structure this presentation? I could start off with some details about the Amazon. But what do I include? No, maybe I'll start with the hospital ship. That's more interesting. No, no. He shook his head.

He rose from the desk and walked over to the window and looked out. He stared for several minutes. God, he thought, how in the world do I approach this? I know about the first three POWs but I'm at a loss in determining what else to do. What should I do?

On returning to the desk, he started typing some bullet lists about the Amazon.

```
┌─────────────────────────────────────────────────────┐
│           BASIC FACTS ABOUT THE AMAZON                │
│                                                       │
│   ●  Hard to predict economy                          │
│   ●  Warm climate                                     │
│   ●  Telephoning is expensive                         │
│   ●  Poor sewage systems                              │
│   ●  Life expectancy is 35 to 50 years                │
│   ●  High infant mortality rate                       │
│   ●  About eleven million people                      │
│   ●  Jungle topsoil is poor for growing crops         │
│   ●  Is approximately the size of the continental     │
│      USA.                                             │
│   ●  Tropical diseases (malaria is the worst)         │
│                                                       │
└─────────────────────────────────────────────────────┘
```

Then he recorded some features about the hospital ship.

```
┌─────────────────────────────────────────────────────┐
│              HOSPITAL SHIP FEATURES                   │
│                                                       │
│   ●  Needs 30 to 50 full-time physicians              │
│   ●  Refurbished cargo vessel                         │
│   ●  Ship load and stabilizers                        │
│   ●  Power sources and back-up generator              │
│   ●  Up-to-date medical equipment                     │
│   ●  Patient rooms                                    │
│   ●  Critical care units                              │
│   ●  Ship maintenance and crew                        │
│   ●  Sterility requirements area                      │
│   ●  Self-supporting                                  │
│                                                       │
└─────────────────────────────────────────────────────┘
```

Finally, he wrote some basic requirements to make the project
a success.

```
┌─────────────────────────────────────────────┐
│              BASIC REQUIREMENTS               │
│                                               │
│   ●  Gain trust of Amazon people              │
│   ●  Gain upper management commitment         │
│   ●  Obtain adequate resources (people, time, │
│      money, equipment, materials and supplies)│
│   ●  Hire a dedicated staff                   │
│   ●  Offer incentives to draw a staff ('chance of a │
│      lifetime')                               │
│   ●  Call attention to this critical international effort │
│   ●  Coordinate effort with Brazilian government │
│   ●  Hire a programme manager                 │
│   ●  Cut red tape for the health and well-being of │
│      the children                             │
│   ●  Prepare for the worst                    │
│                                               │
└─────────────────────────────────────────────┘
```

That was all the information he could muster from his weary brain. He then rose from the desk and went into the living room where his mother sat watching the television.

'What are you watching, mom?'

'My favourite talk show', she said nonchalantly. It was obvious that she was paying more attention to the television programme than to him.

'What's it about?' David wanted to talk to someone, anyone, just to get his mind off the presentation.

'This guy has three wives across the country. The wives are meeting for the first time.'

'Where is he?'

'He decided not to attend.' Her eyes remained glued to the television.

'Mom, what do you like about these shows?'

'Son, talk to me later. I'm watching my show.'

'I need to know.'

She turned toward him and with a growl said, 'Don't you need to work on your presentation?'

'Mom, I already did.'

'Okay, if you need to know, the show presents lots of emotion, it's well organized, and deals with truth. Happy now?'

'You know, I think I need to go and polish up my presentation', he said, heading back to his study.

# Chapter 13

David pulled the manila folder from under his arm and opened it. He handed a copy of his presentation to Demosthenes.

The Greek orator sat silent as he studied the three pages and nibbled on *kasseri*.[1]

A long tedious silence ensued. David felt all the same symptoms he had experienced in front of the people in the park. The dry throat. Faintness. 'Butterflies' in the stomach. Sweaty palms and forehead. Just plain, good old-fashioned fear.

Demosthenes cleared his throat and spat a pebble into the small empty glass next to him on the table.

David couldn't wait to speak. 'Well?'

'What do you think?' asked the Greek in a sullen voice.

'You don't like it?'

'Let's just say, *poulaki mou*, that if you had to give the presentation tomorrow before the New Projects Council I would poison you as they poisoned me. Right now.' He shook his head. 'I've got a lot to teach you and you've got a lot to learn.'

---

[1]*Kasseri*: a mild Greek cheese.

The words cut through David like a hot knife through butter. 'Then', he said, 'there's no hope.'

Demosthenes pushed his head up. 'There's always hope. You'll come through this. But you need to learn about the next POW.'

'I do? What is it, Demosthenes?'

The Greek raised his index finger. 'Not so fast, *poulaki mou*. Not so fast.' He lowered his hand. 'Let's first cover three fundamentals that any presentation must address.' He gave a deep sigh. 'Are you ready to learn about the next POW?'

David nodded his head.

'Good. Now take notes.'

David pulled out a notepad and a pen. He rolled the pen in his hand.

'Stop that', ordered Demosthenes. 'That's a distracting mannerism.'

'Ah … right.' David stopped.

'The contents of every presentation contain the following three fundamentals. Here's a hint. They deal with logic, emotion and truth.'

'Sounds like a talk show to me.'

'A what?'

'A talk show, just like my mom watches. She said it deals with logic, emotion and truth.'

'I see. Well then, using that example, let's go ahead and define them. I'll tell you the first one, because, *poulaki mou*, you need it badly.' Demosthenes spat a pebble into the glass. 'It's called *logos*.'

A bell rang in David's head. He remembered the late night documentary on great speakers. 'You must have used a lot of that in your Philippics.'

'That's right. It means, quite simply, logic. Specifically the organizational structure of the presentation.'

'Like what?' asked David. The bleak outlook now seemed brighter.

'Patience, my friend, patience.' Demosthenes spat another pebble into the glass. 'Then there's *pathos*.'

'*Pathos?*' David sat back into his chair and rubbed his chin as he concentrated. 'Doesn't that have something to do with emotion?'

Demosthenes' eyes widened. David smiled, knowing all too well that he had caught the orator off guard.

'Excellent', said Demost. 'It deals with the emotional content of the presentation. In other words, motivating the audience.'

'Such as?' asked David.

'Patience, I said. Patience.' The Greek spat another pebble into the glass. 'The third one deals with *ethos*.'

'With what?' David wrestled with the word for a second or two and then blurted an answer. 'Oh, I know. It's something like a universal spiritual force that resides in everything. The Egyptians believed in it. But what has that got to do with presentations?'

Demosthenes chuckled.

'What's so funny?' David asked.

'It's got nothing to do with ether', said the Greek. 'It deals with ethics. You know, being truthful, not religious.'

David dropped his chin like a little boy with his feelings hurt.

'So', continued Demosthenes, 'what did you learn?'

'That the contents of all presentations contain three elements', said David, looking up at Demosthenes. '*Logos. Pathos. Ethos.*'

'Good. And remember that preparing a presentation involves considering the use of *logos*, *pathos* and *ethos*', said Demosthenes. 'Now you're ready for a comprehensive lesson on *logos*. And when I'm done, you'll turn into a premier sophist, a master logician.'

# Chapter 14

The Greek orator climbed on to the stage in the lounge. He reached behind a curtain and brought out a three-legged stand holding a pad of paper. 'Now, let's get to grips with *logos*.'

'Okay with me', David said. He tapped his fingers on the table top.

'Please stop tapping your fingers', he said. 'It distracts me.'

'Sorry.' David placed his hands on his lap.

'Now *logos* deals with just what the word implies, logic. And logic implies structure and reasoning', said Demosthenes with a sigh. 'I noticed that the presentation you prepared for the New Projects Council lacks both. Let's talk about structure first. Okay, what's the first item missing?'

'A ... ah ... '

'Here's a clue', said Demost. 'It's what most books start off with.'

'Let's see ... I know', said David, smiling. 'An introduction.'

'That's right. And what follows an introduction?'

'The details?'

'You're correct again. Only we call it the main body.'

'I see. It's like the chapters in a book', said David. 'It contains the details of what the presentation is all about.'

'Very good, *poulaki mou*. Now what follows the main body?'

'Well, based on the logic of what you have told me so far', noted David, 'I'd say it's the summary.'

'You're sort of right again. Only it's called the conclusion.' Demosthenes spat a pebble into a spittoon at the base of the curtain near the podium. 'Let's discuss each part of the presentation in greater detail.'

'Sounds logical to me', said David with a chuckle.

'Cute, but it won't be a laughing matter when you talk in front of the New Projects Council.'

David's smile disappeared.

Demosthenes wrote 'Introduction' at the top of the paper. 'The introduction? What's its purpose?'

'To introduce the subject!'

'How witty. Any other brilliant insights?'

'Hmm … let's see.' David stroked his chin. 'I know! It's to indicate the purpose of the presentation.'

'Give the man a cigar', said Demosthenes as he rolled his eyes skyward. He then wrote that answer on the paper. 'What else?'

'I'd say it establishes parameters on what the presentation covers and … ' said David, snapping his fingers, 'doesn't cover.'

'Excellent.' Demost wrote 'scope'. 'Now above all else, it must grab the listeners' attention.' He wrote 'attention-getter'. 'We'll discuss that further when we talk about *pathos*, next.'

'Okay.' David felt more confident. 'I guess we're ready to discuss the main body?'

'That sounds like a logical progression to me', said Demosthenes. He flipped to the next blank page on the pad and wrote 'Main body' on it. 'Now, what can you tell me about the main body?'

David wrestled in his mind for an answer. But he could only say that it contained detailed information about the topic.

'You're right', said Demost. 'But the detailed information includes the main ideas contained within the presentation. The main body, however, is not a hodgepodge of ideas.' He wrote these words: 'logical flow'. Then he said, 'The ideas must follow some logical flow or sequence. This flow might be based on a number of factors like ... '

'Chronology', interrupted David.

'Very good. And ... '

'Spatiality.'

'Good. There are others but the important point is that the ideas are tied together by one theme. I can see you're thinking like a pro now. What are some other ways to connect ideas?'

'Maybe part to whole', said David. 'Such as describing the way to build a house.'

'Good. Good.'

'From simple to complex.'

'Very good.'

'Or cause and effect.'

'You're hot.'

'Maybe even problem to solution.'

'You're burning, *poulaki mou*.'

'Even known to unknown', said David, falling back into his chair. He felt his temples pound.

'As they say in opera, magnifico.' Demost applauded. 'Okay, enough of past glories. Let's discuss conclusion.'

'Yes, let's', said David, feeling more confident, almost arrogant.

'How about me running the show here?' said Demost.

'Ah ... right.' David restrained himself. 'The conclusion, I guess, summarizes the main ideas.'

'Excellent.' Demosthenes released a proud smile. 'You're still talking like a pro. There are, of course, other things to include in the conclusion. But these deal with *pathos*, our next topic. For now, I'll just write down "conclusion" and underneath "summary of main ideas".'

'This was a lot easier than I thought', said David with a returning smile.

'That's right. All you have to do is think logically, look at a presentation consisting of three main sequential parts ... '

'The introduction, which defines the purpose and scope', said David.

'Right, and ... '

'The main body which presents ideas in a logical flow.'

'That's it. Don't stop ... '

'And then the conclusion which summarizes the main ideas.'

'Bravo! Now if that was so easy why didn't you structure your presentation that way?'

David hesitated and said, 'I don't know. I guess I just wasn't thinking ... logically.'

Demosthenes smiled. 'Let's discuss briefly the other part of *logos*, reasoning.'

'Sure', said David, nodding eagerly.

'All ideas should be supported by facts, data and examples. It strengthens your ideas.'

'Can you back up that idea?' asked David.

'Cute, *poulaki mou*. Real cute.' Demosthenes continued. 'You can use the facts, data and examples in two ways. One way is to show the facts, data and examples first and then present the idea.'

'That's called inductive reasoning', said David.

'Excellent, *poulaki mou*. Then there's the other way. You first present the idea, next the facts, data and examples and return to the idea one more time, if necessary.'

'That's called deductive reasoning', said David.

'You catch on quickly.' Demosthenes then spat a pebble into the spittoon. 'Ready for the next lesson?'

# Chapter 15

'Now let's discuss the three parts of a presentation from the perspective of *pathos*', said Demosthenes as he turned the pages on the flipchart back to 'Introduction'. 'Can you recall what *pathos* is?'

David thought for a second. 'Yeah. It deals with motivating the audience to pay attention and be receptive to your ideas. It means grabbing their heart.'

'Exactly.' Demosthenes then stepped forward to emphasize his next point. 'The introduction, although it takes up only about ten per cent of a presentation, sets the stage for the audience's receptivity to what you have to say. That means what?'

'Hmmm ... Let's see', mumbled David. 'It means you must be clear.'

'Yes. But ... '

'Concise ... '

'Yes ... '

'Audible.'

'Yes, but ... ' David tossed his hands in the air. 'Well then, I don't know.'

'Attention', said Demosthenes. 'You have to gain their attention. And quickly. Otherwise, no one will listen to you. You might as well lock yourself in a room and talk to yourself.'

'You're right', agreed David. 'You need to gain their attention.'

Demosthenes spat a pebble into the spittoon. 'It's like a novel. The first few pages must capture your attention or you'll never read the entire book.'

'But what is an attention-getter?'

Demosthenes started writing on the paper as he spoke. 'I want you to guess them. I'll give you one answer to get the juices flowing. Starting off with a provocative question is one way to gain attention.'

'Yeah, I see. You could also tell a story', added David. 'Or make a profound or startling statement. Maybe even give a demonstration.' He watched as the Greek orator jotted on the paper each answer. 'Use a quotation. Or even mention a single word.'

Demosthenes scribbled quickly across the paper. He then spat a pebble. 'Attention-getters must be used very carefully.'

'How so?' asked David.

'If they're not related to the main idea of the presentation then they detract from what you have to say and you do not achieve the desired effect.'

David sat upright in his chair. 'There's other complications, too. You could offend someone if it's not done tastefully.'

'Very good, *poulaki mou*.' Demosthenes stepped forward. 'And it had better be synchronized with your delivery style.'

'Oh?'

'Well, for example, if you are a structured, low-key type of presenter, you might avoid telling a loud, risqué joke. People will just think you're faking it to gain their attention.'

'I see.'

'Regardless of what you do to engage attention, you need to answer WIIFM.'

'Answer what?' asked David.

'It's an acronym. It stands for What's In It For Me? If you don't answer that question you'll lose your audience. The answer might be financial, emotional, spiritual, whatever.' Demosthenes scratched WIIFM on the paper. He then flipped the introduction page and turned to the one on the main body. 'Enough about the introduction. Now let's discuss the main body and *pathos*.'

David felt more confident than ever. He placed his feet on the table and put his hands behind his head. 'Go ahead.'

'Thank you. You're very kind', snapped Demosthenes. 'Incorporating *pathos* in the main body requires just as much talent as having it in the introduction.' He spat a pebble into the spittoon. 'The difference is that it requires providing emotional support for your ideas. That means what?'

David pulled his hands down and his feet off the table. 'I guess it means supporting your ideas in specific ways that hit them right here.' He tapped the left side of his chest.

'What are some?'

'You could use statistics or other data to support your ideas but in a way that engages their emotional support.'

Demosthenes started scribbling. 'What else?'

'You can use examples … facts … even personal experience.'

'Hold on', Demosthenes said as he wrote.

David grimaced, waiting anxiously to show off his knowledge. 'Oh okay, continue.'

'You can use values, beliefs, demonstrations … and testimonials.'

'Excellent. But you forgot one. An ancient friend of mine in another distant culture said a picture is worth a thousand words.'

'I know who that was', said David. 'It was Confucius. I know what you're saying, too. You're saying use exhibits, graphics, diagrams and charts.'

'Very good, *poulaki mou*. It helps visualize what you're saying. Seventy-five per cent of the world is visually oriented. That means most people relate more easily to pictures than to written words or what they hear. A picture that touches the heart can do more than a litany of facts and data. It's less abstract. More immediate.'

David nodded.

Demosthenes scratched diagrams on the paper and then flipped to the next page. 'Now let's talk about *pathos* and the conclusion.'

'Fair enough.' David couldn't wait to get started on his presentation.

'Good. Now remind me about the purpose of the conclusion.'

'It summarizes the main ideas of the presentation.'

'Right. But from a *pathos* perspective, it rouses the audience to action. In other words … '

'In other words', interrupted David, 'it capitalizes on their receptivity by encouraging them to do something.'

'You can do that by including a story, illustration, statistic – whatever works for you.' The Greek wrote his answers. 'Like the introduction, it takes ten per cent of the total presentation and must keep people's attention. Like a novel, it functions like the last chapter or epilogue, putting everything into place. But it does one thing more.'

'What's that?'

'Your brain activity must be slowing down. I just told you the answer. It rouses to action. Encourages people to do something with what you said.' Demosthenes spat into the spittoon but nothing came from his mouth. He then reached into his pockets and pulled out some pebbles. He tossed them into his mouth, one by one. 'That about wraps up our conversation on *pathos*. Now let's talk about the next subject.'

# Chapter 16

'So what about *ethos*?' asked David.

Demosthenes stepped away from the flipchart stand and spat a pebble squarely into the spittoon. 'Now why don't you refresh my memory on what *ethos* is.'

David nodded. 'Okay. It deals with the truthfulness of what you say. You know, speaking honestly. You know, not being deceptive.'

'You mean having … ' Demosthenes walked back to the stand and flipped to a clean sheet and said as he wrote, 'credibility.'

'Yeah, that's the word.'

'What are ways to establish and build credibility with your audience? In other words, what makes you an expert?' Demosthenes stood ready to write the answers.

'Let's see … I know … One way is to present yourself to the audience.'

'In what ways?'

'Not appearing pompous or arrogant.'

Demosthenes started to write.

'Not ridiculing or insulting members of the audience', added David.

'Don't forget the entire audience as well.'

'Right', said David. He leaned forward in his chair. 'Or using sarcasm.'

'What else? Such as personal appearance?'

'Oh yeah. You need to have a clean, well-groomed appearance. Tie straight and shoes shined.'

'Anything else?' asked Demosthenes in a weak voice.

David caught on right away. 'I know. Speak clearly and in a way that projects your confidence in what you talk about.'

'What about this?' Demosthenes then crossed his arms across his chest.

David snapped his fingers as he spoke. 'You need to project positive, supporting body language.'

'And ... ' Demosthenes pointed to his eyes.

'You need to maintain good eye contact.'

Demosthenes spat a pebble into the spittoon as he stopped writing. 'You see, *ethos* has a lot to do with trusting that what you say is accurate. It's important how you carry yourself through the entire presentation, from the introduction, through the main body, and to the conclusion. That means having *philotempo*, which is Greek for having a sense of honour and self-respect. And even though it ties closely with the first POW, Perception, it's important in this POW we are currently discussing. So what are some things about the material itself to enhance its veracity as well as the credibility of the presenter?'

'The presentation should be understandable to the audience', said David, falling back into his chair and putting his hands behind his neck. 'The question is, how?'

Demosthenes flipped to a clean page and started to write. 'One way is to avoid packing the presentation with statistics.'

'Yeah, that only confuses people. Worse, it bores them.'

'Another way', continued Demosthenes, 'is to use short quotes, not lengthy ones. Lengthy quotes, let alone too many, make people think you don't have a mind of your own or that you're avoiding or hiding something.'

'Yeah, I remember a presentation like that where ... '

'Save the war stories for later', said Demosthenes. 'Still another way is to avoid jargon.'

'And pretentious language that nobody understands.'

'That's correct, *poulaki mou*.' Demosthenes popped a pebble into his mouth and spat it into the spittoon. 'That only obfuscates the listeners.'

'Huh?' David sat upright. 'Ob ... Ob ... Ob ... '

Demosthenes took a pebble from his pocket and tossed it to David. 'Put that in your mouth. It'll help stop the stuttering. The word is obfuscate', repeated the Greek. 'It means confusing people.' Demosthenes then smiled as he asked, 'Ain't there no more things?'

'Demost, that's bad grammar.'

'That's precisely my point. You want to use good grammar that contains the active voice and as little wordiness as possible. You can start by eliminating excessive adjectives and adverbs.'

'I absolutely positively agree.' David thought the Greek would catch the redundant comment.

But Demosthenes continued to record the insights. Finished, he said, 'That's an exhaustive list. We'll discuss many of these later when we talk about delivery. But for now, that's it. I'm growing tired.' A pebble fell from his lips and hit the floor.

'But what about visual aids?'

'What about them?' Demosthenes sighed and flipped to a clean page and prepared to write more. 'All right, fair enough. But that's it for tonight. *Logos*, *pathos* and *ethos* all apply as well. Remember that. But visual aids need extra care and effort or they can backfire. They must all share some common characteristics. What do you think are some of them?' He wrote 'visual aids' at the top.

'They must be clear to the audience', said David.

Demosthenes scribbled. 'Good. Good. What else?'

'Relevant to the topic you're presenting', David said after taking a deep breath. 'They also must be understandable to the audience.'

'What about from the perspective of the presenter?'

'Well, they must be easy to use. You don't want to become confused when using them during the presentation.'

'That's right.' Demosthenes struggled to spit a pebble and managed to do so with considerable effort. He then raised his finger as he made this point: 'Remember, *poulaki mou*, visual aids should aid, I repeat aid, the presentation, and not vice versa.'

'Wow, Demosthenes, that's a good point.'

'That's why I'm writing it down. Now try to guess what types of visual aid you can use.'

'Let's see ... yeah, I know. I can use a slide projector ... overhead projector ... '

Demosthenes continued to write.

'I can use white or blackboards ... flipcharts just like you, Demost ... computer slide shows if I really want to be hi-tech ... video and audio cassettes ... real objects or models or mock-ups, I guess ... That's about it, I think ... '

Demosthenes wrote the last item. 'Very good, *poulaki mou*. I think that is about it for now.'

David felt that he had just begun. 'But Demosthenes, I have questions about other topics, like delivering the material.'

'Look', said Demosthenes, ripping off the handwritten pages from the flipchart and carrying them down to David's table. 'I'm an old man. I need my rest. What you can do is take the information I gave you and develop a good copy of your presentation for the New Projects Council. I'll see you tomorrow night at eight to continue our lesson.'

'But ... '

Before David could say anything more, Demosthenes called for Demetri, the same strong man who had rushed David out before.

'And if you don't leave, I'll have him hold you down while I spit pebbles at you.'

David quickly rolled up his notes, placed them under his arm and hurried out of the front door.

# Chapter 17

After a good night's sleep, David woke early and started working. From under the door of his study he could smell the cooking of eggs and bacon.

Mom always treats me right when the pressure's on, he thought. Painstakingly, he taped the flipchart sheets on the walls. After taping the last sheet, he walked over to the calendar on his desk and noticed that he had two more days until his presentation before the New Projects Council. He highlighted that day in fluorescent red.

It's getting closer, he thought. All the symptoms of standing in front of an audience returned to him. He paced around the room like a mountain lion in a cage. He looked up at the walls and screamed inside: What do I do next? How do I get started?

He heard a gentle knock and watched the door creak open. 'What?'

His mother walked in and laid the tray on his desk. She looked at the walls. 'Not my choice of wallpaper. But you're a grown man.'

He pointed to the meal. 'Thanks, mom. But I'm not hungry.'

'Son, you need your strength. Take five minutes to eat your food. You'll gain strength and at the same time let the recesses of your mind decide what you need to do.'

'Okay, okay', he said. 'You're right. Absolutely right.' He sat at his desk and ate. 'You know', he said as he chewed his food, 'I now understand why you like that talk show you watch every day. It is well organized, catches your emotions, and is honest and direct. I understand now.'

'Son, I didn't mean to snap at you. But at my age that show is the big highlight of my day.' She kissed his cheek and headed towards the door. She turned and said, 'You've just got to have the same impact on your listeners. You need to make them feel the same way.' She closed the door behind her.

She's right, he thought. I've got to make them feel the same way. It may not be the highlight of their day but it can be the best presentation they ever heard.

He finished his breakfast and fell back in his chair as he closed his eyes and let himself visualize how he would like the presentation to go.

He saw himself standing next to an overhead projector facing a panel of five people. They were gazing up at the projector. No, at the image on the screen. No, at him! His heart raced. Yet he sounded confident as he watched the earnest look on their faces. Then came questions and at the end applause. Yeah, he thought, that's how I want it to go.

If it can go that well, I will surely make it to the next step, giving a presentation before the Executive Steering Committee.

He opened his eyes and looked around the room. Reality hit him square in the face. There's a long way to go towards making that dream come true, he thought.

He pushed the tray aside and opened a paper pad, took up a pen and scribbled on a single sheet:

I.     *Introduction*
    *A.  Purpose*
    *B.  Scope*

He then added:

II.    *Background*
III.   *Proposal*
IV.    *Benefits*
V.     *Requirements*
VI.    *Conclusion*

Finally, he remembered to add:

VII.  *Next Steps*

    Fine, he thought. It may not be perfect but it's a start. He made sure in his mind and then from the mindset of the audience that his structure had a logical flow to it. *Logos*, he thought.

    'First, I'll start with the introduction', he mumbled. On a separate sheet he wrote:

I.     *INTRODUCTION*
    *Purpose*
    *Scope*

Then he wrote each of the following on a separate sheet in capital letters:

II.    *BACKGROUND*
III.   *PROPOSAL*
IV.    *BENEFITS*
V.     *REQUIREMENTS*
VI.    *CONCLUSION*
VII.  *NEXT STEPS*

For each one, he noted detailed information. The whole process took about two hours of intensive thought, rummaging through books and magazines that he had collected to compile the presentation. 'There, that should do it', he mumbled. Yet he felt an uneasiness, a dissatisfaction with what he had produced. Somehow, and in some way, the presentation seemed incomplete.

'Mom!' he cried. He waited several long seconds. Then he heard the creak of the door.

'Yes, son?'

'Mom. I need your help.'

'Deciding who to marry?' she asked, closing the door behind her.

'No, mom. It's not that.' He handed her the pad. 'Mom, I need you to tell me what you think about what I've written.'

'I don't know anything about giving a presentation, son. I ... '

'Mom, listen.' He put his arm around her. 'I just need someone to look at what I did. That's all.'

She scanned the pages. 'Looks like a lot of stuff. Are you going to present it this way? As a set of wrinkled pages?'

'No, no. I'm going to list them on a slide. One slide per section.'

'Oh my', she said. 'I don't understand why you broke it down this way.'

'Well, according to Demost ... '

'Demosthenes? You call him Demost? How cute ... '

'Yes, mom. He said that a presentation has three fundamental contents. *Logos. Pathos. Ethos.*'

'Huh?'

'I'll explain. Remember when I interrupted you while you were glued to your talk show?'

'Yeah?'

'You said it was well organized?'

'And ... '

'Well, mom, that's *logos*, meaning there's a logical structure to the presentation.'

'I see.' She looked through the papers once more. 'The material does seem to flow logically.'

'Great. Then you said that your show involves you emotionally, by making you want to watch.'

'Ah huh.'

'That's *pathos*. It involves your connection with the speaker. Even sympathy.'

'Oh dear. I think I understand.'

'And then you said that the show deals with the truth. That it deals with subjects truthfully.'

'Yes.'

'That's called *ethos*.' He took a deep breath. 'What do you think?'

A long pause ensued as she gave one further perusal of the material. 'I think it has *log … log …* '

'*Logos*, mom.'

'Yes, that's it. I also think it has *ethos* because I know my son would never tell a lie.' She tilted her head and gave him a warm smile. 'But I have to tell you one thing.'

'What's that, mom?'

'All these lists look boring. I don't find anything you wrote here exciting.'

'What?'

'It looks like a grocery list. You need something that would excite the listeners. It just looks like a giant checklist.'

David fell back in his chair. His mom came over and rubbed his forehead. 'I hurt your feelings, didn't I?'

'No, mom.'

'Yes I did. I'd better not mention something else.'

'What is it, mom?' he asked, staring straight into her eyes.

'Well … you promise not to get hurt or angry?'

'I promise', he said with a sigh. 'What is it?'

'It's logical. But I need to see something somewhere that tells me what you expect to cover in the presentation. I feel as if I'm being led through a mall without any sense of direction. For all I know, I could end up in a flea market rather than a high-class retail store.'

'But it has an introduction, a main body and a conclusion. What more direction do you need?'

'No, son, it's not what more direction *I* need. It's what more direction *you* need. I suggest you bring the matter up with Demost! As for me', she continued, as she looked up at the clock on the wall, 'it's time to watch my talk show.'

# Chapter 18

Demosthenes began reviewing David's copy of the presentation as he sipped coffee. He also played with a pebble in his mouth as he glanced at the first page.

---

**Love is for Everyone Proposal**


**October 27, 19XX**


**David Michaels**

---

He looked at David. 'I see you have a title page', said the Greek. 'That's good.'

David smiled.

Demosthenes returned his attention to the copy and flipped to the next page.

---

## I.  INTRODUCTION

### A.  PURPOSE

To build a hospital facility site
and a complementary hospital ship
to go up and down the Amazon River Basin.

---

'You have an introduction stating the purpose. Good.' He looked at the next page.

---

## I.  INTRODUCTION

### B.  SCOPE

To provide trained medical staff,
sufficient medicines, state-of-the-art
technology and modern equipment to
health-impaired children.

---

'The introduction also has a scope. Excellent, *poulaki mou*.' He turned the page.

---

## II.  BACKGROUND

A.  The Yuggenheim Foundation was established in 1899, almost 100 years ago. Since that time it has taken the lead in philanthropic endeavours in commercial industry.

B.  At this time the foundation is interested in South American activities.

---

David started feeling very confident.

'You give some background information', Demosthenes noted as he flipped to the next page.

---

## III.  PROPOSAL

A.  To build a modern hospital structure which provides all necessary treatments and services and maintains the highest standards of medical care.

B.  Do the same as above for the hospital ship.

---

'You then present your proposal. Not a bad approach.' He turned the page.

---

### IV.   BENEFITS

The Yuggenheim Foundation

A.   Gain additional significant universal recognition for its humanitarian efforts.

B.   Marketing of the foundation's name would be greatly enhanced.

---

'You list the benefits to the Yuggenheim Foundation', the Greek said. 'Good move.' He proceeded to the next page.

---

### IV.   BENEFITS

The Brazilian Government

A.   A boost in economy in addition to improved medical treatments and services.

B.   An opportunity for a joint venture with a foreign mega-corporation.

---

'And to the Brazilian government, I see. On the next page you identify requirements.'

---

### V.   REQUIREMENTS


A.   To start up this endeavour requires identifying a programme manager to direct the programme and form a cadre team to coordinate and lead the activities.

B.   Financial arrangements must be made.

---

'That's followed by a conclusion', observed Demosthenes.

## VI.  CONCLUSION

A.  The Love is for Everyone Project payback is many-fold. There are improved opportunities for:

- Products and services to be made known
- Tax write-offs
- Joint venture opportunities.

B.  There are intangible opportunities which include:

- Promoting a planet that works together
- Yuggenheim Foundation initiatives will be viewed as a standard of excellence for other organizations.

'And lastly', he said as he skimmed the final page, 'you list what follow-up actions are necessary.'

## VII.   NEXT STEPS

### The New Projects Council

A.   Obtain go-ahead to give explanatory presentation to the Executive Steering Committee.

Demosthenes sat silent for what seemed forever to David. The Greek then spoke. 'It appears to have good logical structure. You have an introduction, a main body and a conclusion. Very good.'

'*Logos*', said David softly.

'That's right.' Demosthenes stroked his chin. 'Each of the main points has supporting detail that adds weight to your cause, such as benefits, that emotionally involves me. The audience should like that.'

'*Pathos*', added David.

'Correct. You have statistics and facts. Good. The main ideas have a logical flow, each leading to the next one. Excellent. The introduction has a purpose. The conclusion summarizes the presentation. Well done. Both the introduction and conclusion together take about twenty per cent of the presentation, each exceeding not more than ten per cent. So far so good, except ... '

'Except?' David shifted his weight in his chair. 'Except what?'

'Well, the purpose of this presentation is to inform. Right?'

David nodded. His heart pounded.

'The presentation does that. But it lacks several things if you hope to get the message across.'

'What's that?'

'It lacks a general picture. What you need, *poulaki mou*, is an agenda.'

'A what?'

'An agenda. You can either start the presentation with one or you can make it part of the introduction. But you need some-where to tell the audience what you intend to talk about. This will fix in their minds what you will discuss and where you are going with the presentation. For you, I'd have a separate page for the agenda, before giving the introduction. Your audience already has some idea what you're going to talk about, right?'

David nodded. 'I guess the way to build an agenda is to present something like this.' He handed the Greek a piece of paper after he had finished scribbling on it.

*AGENDA*
*October 27, 19xx*

| | |
|---|---|
| I. | *Introduction* |
| II. | *Background* |
| III. | *Proposal* |
| IV. | *Benefits* |
| V. | *Requirements* |
| VI. | *Conclusion* |
| VII. | *Next Steps* |

'Excellent. That will give them some idea of how you plan to get from point A to point Z, so to speak.'

David felt his pulse rate decline. 'My mom noticed that I needed something like an agenda.'

Demosthenes' eyes widened. 'She did?'

'Yeah.'

'A very observant woman. I like that about a woman. She sounds like Athena, goddess of wisdom and goddess of the arts.

Anyway, let's talk about your pages. You did right by not having too many items on a page. A good rule of thumb is to have no more than nine items on a page. More than that and the audience will find the page crowded. White space helps to break up the monotony. Also ... '

'Yes?' asked David, nervously.

'Don't be defensive. I'm trying to help you.'

David took a deep breath and nodded.

'Also, make sure the size, the point size of the letters, is large enough for everyone in the audience to see. This is especially the case if you're using slides.'

'I plan to.'

'Then heed the point. And use bullets or some type of symbol, not roman numerals next to each point, just like you did in this agenda and on the slides. For sub-lists, use hyphens, dashes, or some other symbols. The idea is to show the hierarchy of the items.' Demosthenes took a deep breath. 'Now there's one more concern I have, *poulaki mou*.' He spat a pebble into a jar.

'And that is?'

'The presentation is boring. It's all bullet lists. It's like a checklist.'

'My mom said the same thing.'

'She did?' Demosthenes smiled. 'This mom of yours sounds like a very smart lady. Perhaps some day we can meet?'

David was taken off guard. 'Ah, yeah. Sure. Maybe ... '

'I'd be honoured.' Demosthenes coughed. 'Anyway, you need a chart or diagram of some sort to show the visualization of what you want to do.'

'Like what?'

'You're the expert', said Demosthenes. 'You tell me.'

'Well, maybe I can draw a map.'

'That's one idea.'

'Or a schematic diagram of the hospital ship or of the hospital.' David was feeling more confident.

'The requirements for a diagram are that it be uncluttered, understandable and relevant. If you have any diagram that lacks one of these, it will only hinder effective communication, not help it.'

'You know, my mom also said I needed a diagram', said David.

'She did?'

'Yeah.'

'You have a smart mother', said the Greek orator. 'I've never met her but some day I hope to. Perhaps one day you can bring her over to the lounge. The drinks will be on me.'

'Or better yet', said David, 'maybe I can have you over for dinner. She cooks great spaghetti.'

'Ah ... '

'What's the matter, Demost? Not like spaghetti?'

Demosthenes grimaced.

'She also cooks a mean *dolmathes*!'

'I'll be there! I'll bring something to drink.'

David coughed. 'Ah, I still have to ask her.'

'Of course.' Demosthenes turned red. 'Now to one more matter.'

'What's that?'

'You have to think about your mode of delivery.'

'My what?' asked David, squeezing his eyebrows together.

'Mode of delivery. Are you going to use an outline? Note cards? Narrative text?'

'I guess I haven't given it much thought.'

'Well you better, *poulaki mou*. Give it some thought right now by discussing the pros and cons.' Demosthenes spat a pebble into the jar. 'Here's the first question.'

'Ready, sir.' David smiled and gave a mock salute.

'Don't do that, *poulaki mou*,' Demosthenes said as he waved his hand. 'It reminds me too much of King Philip's troops.'

'Sorry.'

'You have four modes of delivery. What are they?'

'I could use an outline.'

'That's one.'

'I could use note cards.'

'That's two.'

'I could use narrative text.'

'That's three.'

'And I guess … Er, I had it on the tip of my tongue … but I can't remember', said David, tapping the side of his head. 'I guess I forgot.'

'The fourth one', said Demosthenes, 'is memory.'

'That's it!' said David.

'Cute. Let's discuss them in reverse order. That means talking about memory first.'

'Using memory is dangerous just for the reason you showed me', said David. 'You can forget. But also if you memorize too much, you appear too rehearsed. You lose your natural style. That can translate into a boring, but polished, presentation. Like appearing as a robot.'

'That's right. However, relying on memory has its positive sides. You avoid fumbling with cards or papers. You also have an opportunity to maintain eye contact with your audience.'

David gulped. 'You mean looking straight at them.'

'That's right.' Demosthenes winked and continued. 'The next mode is narrative text. Having a fully written text of your presentation. You know, like a formal speech.'

'You mean a word-for-word description of what you're going to say.'

'Exactly. It has some positive sides', said Demosthenes. He popped a pebble into his mouth. 'You may feel more confident in what you're saying. You have greater control over what you say because you're sure of what to say.'

'In other words', added David. 'You avoid saying the wrong things or miscommunicating ideas.'

'That's it. But using narrative text requires considerable practice. It's very easy to lose your place. The hard copy or handwritten letters must be big enough so that you don't. It also requires considerable practice to give the appearance that you're not reading ... '

'It also gives the opportunity to stare at the paper and not the audience! Maybe I should use narrative delivery ... '

'I think that's a cop-out, David', said Demosthenes, shaking his head. 'I don't recommend it, especially for that reason. The next mode of delivery is note cards.'

David gave a thumbs-up.

'Note cards are the mode of delivery often recommended in public speaking classes. They have their advantages.'

'They're compact', volunteered David. 'And give you more flexibility in rearranging your notes.'

'Very good, *poulaki mou*. What are some of the problems?'

David thought for several seconds. 'You could drop them during the presentation.'

'That's right. Then you'd have to disrupt the presentation to pick them up and put them back in order. Very tacky and very embarrassing. What else?'

David raised his finger. 'You can only put so much on a card.'

'That's correct. You should only put one idea per card. You need to ensure that the writing is large enough, just like in the narrative format we discussed earlier. What else?'

David scratched his head. 'I should think you'd have to be careful how you use them. The audience could see you flipping one card after another.'

'Exactly. It could become a distracting mannerism as you move from card to card', said Demosthenes. He chuckled and added, 'You could look as if you're bobbing for apples with each flip of the card.'

'That leaves outlines.'

'Yes.' Demosthenes rose from his chair. 'Outlines. They have their advantages. What are … ?'

'One is that they provide a comprehensive view of the presentation as you speak.'

'Good. More?'

'Yeah', David said. 'They're less distracting and cumbersome than note cards.'

'Very good. But what are some of the drawbacks of outlines?' asked Demosthenes.

'Like note cards and narrative text you can lose your place. And if you drop the pages of the outline, you have to stop the presentation.'

'Excellent observation.'

David coughed. 'Then what's best?'

'Only you can determine that. What I recommend is that since you're using slides, each bullet could act as a memory jogger for you to speak from. Or you could write on the slide frames. The writing on the frame won't show through to the screen. But that's your decision. You are giving the presentation, so you pick what's best for you.'

'That might work better', said David. 'But if I decide to use note cards or outlines what can I do to make my presentation better?'

Demosthenes raised his first finger. 'One, you can highlight key words in the presentation. You can use brightly coloured or fluorescent markers, underline words, or use a colour printer for microcomputers.'

'Good idea. What else?'

Demosthenes popped up finger number two. 'You can use a large type on the documents. The twenty-sixth American president, Teddy Roosevelt, considered one of the best speakers of his time, did that.'

'But', said David, 'he was much older than I am.'

Demosthenes grimaced. He spat a pebble and rose a third finger. 'You can use wider spacing between lines. Such as double or triple spacing.'

The Greek stuck up a fourth finger. 'You can also use signposts in the columns to mark where you are at any time during the presentation. These signposts could be special characters, maybe even little symbols that represent an idea or thought.'

'Wow, good stuff', said David.

'Of course. How could you expect anything less?'

'Well, I guess I'd better go make the changes.' David started to rise.

'Not so fast, *poulaki mou*. Not so fast.' Demosthenes spat a pebble into the spittoon. 'You should by now have no trouble telling me the fourth P.'

David eased himself back into his chair. He started to chew on his lower lip. 'Let's see ... The first P is perspective ... the second P is perception ... the third P is planning ... The fourth P is ... '

'I'll give you a guess. It's determining in advance the structure of the presentation, the content, and the layout.'

'That requires a lot of preparation', David said. 'That's it! It's preparation.'

'Excellent. You are very smart, *poulaki mou*.' Demosthenes spat towards the spittoon on the stage but only saliva shot from between his lips. 'I didn't prepare myself for that one very well. Ran out of pebbles. Time to call it a day.'

David agreed. He rose from his chair and headed for home.

# Chapter 19

With the flipchart sheets taped to the walls of his study, David began working on revising his presentation. He drafted an agenda with more detail. He then drafted a map of the Amazon River Basin and highlighted where he planned to locate the hospital and the route the ship would take.

He realized that, although his penmanship and drawing abilities were fine, he needed to convert the material into a readable and understandable form. Handwritten text just would not leave a good impression. He turned to the side of his desk where the rented microcomputer sat and turned on the machine. After a few grunting sounds and beeps software choices flashed on the screen. He accessed the graphics software and started building the pages and diagrams for his presentation. Two hours later, he printed out the presentation and was ready for his next step.

'Mom!' he shouted.

Seconds later, the door creaked open. 'Yes, son?'

'Mom, I need your advice again.'

'Is it about a girl?'

'No, mom', said David, shaking his head. 'It's got nothing to do with a girl. It has to do with my presentation.'

'Oh ... '

He handed her his presentation. He watched as she flipped through the pages. Several minutes slid by until she spoke: 'This is very good. I'm impressed with this, David.'

'Is it logical?'

She nodded.

'Does it make it easy for you to see what I want to do?'

She nodded.

'Does it seem straightforward? You know, communicate in a honest manner?'

She nodded.

'Great', said David. 'What about its appearance?'

'It looks wonderful.' She bent over and kissed him on the fore-head. 'What does Demost think?'

'He likes the general approach. He agreed with what you said earlier. He even said that you were a very smart lady.'

'Oh, he did?' she asked. Her face turned red. 'Well, it does look so much clearer and more understandable.'

'He hasn't seen this polished copy yet. Until now, you two have only seen a handwritten copy.'

'When can I hear you give it?'

'No one else can attend the New Projects Council with me, mom.'

'Aren't you going to have a dry run? It's tomorrow.'

'A what?'

'A dry run, you know, a rehearsal?'

'Goodness, mom, I never thought much about that. There's no time. It's three in the afternoon and the pitch tomorrow is at nine in the morning. I need a rest. I'll just flash up the slides and read from them.'

'You'd better call Demost.'

'But tomorrow is only an informative session. I don't have to explain everything in detail or persuade anyone to do anything, at least not yet.'

She reached for the receiver on his desk and handed it to him. 'Call Demost. Right now.'

# Chapter 20

David paced around in the lounge. He couldn't stop, trying to control the nervousness that seemed to consume him.

'Just sit down', said Demosthenes. 'Relax.'

'I can't. I just can't. I gave no thought to rehearsing this presentation. I just figured that it would be enough to flash the slides on the screen, read a few words, and that would be it.'

Demosthenes stood at the bar sipping *nero* from a liqueur glass. 'Darn good stuff, I must say. It tastes as good now as it did over two thousand years ago.'

'How can you think about water at a time like this?'

'You prefer hemlock?' retorted Demosthenes. 'Look, whoever told you that you need to rehearse deserves a medal. That guy hit the nail on the head.'

David stopped pacing. 'It wasn't a guy. It was my mom.'

'As I said, she's a smart woman. Just like Athena. You should listen to her.' Demosthenes finished his drink and popped some pebbles in his mouth. 'She's right, you know. You need to rehearse. It's important. There's still time. But not much. I'm supposed to open in fifteen minutes.' He looked at his watch and then signalled to Demetri. 'Draw the blinds and lock the door. We're closed for the evening.'

David fell into a chair.

Demosthenes sat at the table. 'Your slides are great. You've come a long way. But you need to go further. Much further. I'll teach you the basics of the next P, and you can leave here and practise by yourself or with a friend. Okay?'

David released a loud sigh. 'Demost ... you're great!'

'Please, please.' The Greek rose from his chair and walked on to the stage. He then pulled the flipchart stand from behind the curtain. 'First, you need to see the benefits of rehearsals.'

'Whatever you say', said David.

'The most important benefit of a rehearsal is that it builds self-confidence. That means it helps you to conquer stage fright.' Demosthenes scribbled away.

'I'm convinced already', said David. 'Can I pour myself some ouzo?'

'Be my guest.'

David ran to the bar and snatched a liqueur glass and a bottle of ouzo.

'Another benefit is to help you direct your nervous energy by determining what parts of the presentation you want to direct that energy into.'

'You mean focusing it', said David, taking a sip.

'Exactly', said Demosthenes, spitting a pebble into a spittoon. 'A rehearsal helps you to smooth out the rough edges ... '

'You mean', interrupted David, 'like synchronizing your physical actions with the content?'

'That's right.' Demosthenes continued to write. 'It enables you to give a more natural delivery rather than one that appears contrived.'

'You don't want to appear phony.' David took another sip, only this time a bigger one.

'Along with a smoother delivery comes detecting distracting mannerisms.'

'Like jingling change in your pocket or waving a pointer around like a sword.'

'You catch on quickly.' Demosthenes gave David a disapproving look as he wrote on the flipchart. 'You're drinking too much.'

David had begun pouring more liqueur into the glass. 'This will be my last glass.'

The Greek said nothing. He continued to speak as David sipped. 'A rehearsal allows you to learn your material. You know, you never learn your material unless you rehearse it. By speaking the content out loud, you reinforce in your subconscious what you have to say.' Demosthenes continued to write. 'You become more natural in your style, your timing becomes better, and you focus on communicating what you say and how you say it.'

'There's one other benefit you forgot about', said David.

'And that is?'

'You learn to use visual aids better.' David took another sip.

'Excellent', said Demosthenes. 'So you see, rehearsing is a way to help you look, feel and sound good.'

David lifted his liqueur glass in the air. 'Just like a shot of ouzo!'

Demosthenes took a deep breath. He spat a pebble towards David's hand. The pebble smashed right into the glass, shattering it.

'What the … ?'

'You've had too much', warned Demosthenes. 'The next time is right between the eyes.'

David laid the stem of the glass on the table. With his voice trembling, he asked: 'How do I rehearse?'

'I'm glad you asked that question.' Demosthenes turned to the next page and started to write. 'One way is to go to the place where you'll be presenting and rehearse there.'

'I can't do that. It's at a corporate headquarters. Only selected people can get in and at certain times.'

Demosthenes scribbled and then added, 'Then you can rehearse in an environment that resembles the real place.'

'But I've never been in the room where I'll give it.'

Demosthenes spat a pebble into the spittoon.

David jerked in his chair. 'I thought you were … '

'Good. You're alert.' Demosthenes continued to write as he spoke. 'Then you can rehearse in front of a mirror but there's a problem with that. What is it?'

'You only improve body movements.'

'Exactly. And what about with a tape recorder?'

'You can only improve your oral presentation.'

'Keep going. What else is there?'

'A camcorder. That's it. A camcorder. I can tape myself and then review the videotape. I can see myself as others do. That's the ticket. But, I probably will need a tripod … '

'Do you have one handy?' asked Demost.

'Ah … no. I plan to get one. But for now, I guess that's out', sighed David.

'I see the alcohol hasn't killed your brain cells. Well, David, that leaves only one other way to rehearse. What is it?'

'In front of friends and relatives.'

'Right again, *poulaki mou*. Right again. So who might that be in your case?'

'My mom.'

'Just her?'

'Maybe … ah … you … too?'

'Together?'

David smiled. 'Sure, together. All three of us. I'll give her a call. Maybe you can come over for dinner.'

'I'd be delighted', said Demosthenes. 'Can I bring anything? Perhaps olives? Ouzo?'

# Chapter 21

All three sat around the dinner table. David rose from the table, picked up the bottle, and poured ouzo into their delicate liqueur glasses. He then sat.

'An excellent meal, if I must say so myself. It reminds me a lot of ambrosia', said Demosthenes.

'Oh, why thank you', said David's mother. 'It's nothing, really.'

'No. I mean exactly what I said. And to have such a sumptuous meal with such very pleasant company is more than I could hope ever to get in my home country.'

'Yeah', said David. 'He's from Greece.'

'David has told me a lot about you. From Athens, I suspect?'

Demosthenes smiled and nodded his head. 'That is correct.' He raised his right arm, holding the liqueur glass. 'To Athens. How I miss her. Or, I should say, miss her as she was.'

'What happened?' asked David. 'It's still there, isn't it?'

'Ah yes, *poulaki mou*. But not the Athens I knew of yester-year. The Acropolis is now a pile of rubble, fallen columns that delight the visitor of today but wound the heart of an old resident like me.'

David noticed Demosthenes' watery eyes.

'And the Parthenon, truly a wonder of the ancient world and a temple to our gods, is now a monument to what ancient Greece stood for. Freedom! Expression! Liberty! All that was sacred to Athenians.'

David's mother burst into tears. 'Oh dear', she said, wiping her eyes. 'I didn't mean to … '

Demosthenes stared at her. 'Nothing gains my respect more than an intelligent, beautiful lady filled with compassion. Our goddess of love, Aphrodite, would be proud, indeed!' He drank a toast to David's mother. 'Few women have the wisdom of Athena and the beauty of Aphrodite. To a lovely lady. *Yiassas!*'[1]

David followed suit.

'Oh dear. Why thank you, Demosthenes', she said. 'What happened?'

'It was history, Mrs Michaels.'

'Elizabeth. But you can call me Liz.'

'Liz. Ah yes. A name that somehow reminds me of Aphrodite. What a sweet lady she was.'

Liz blushed.

David felt he needed to move the conversation forward. 'Well anyway, what happened?'

'Disaster', said Demosthenes. 'First came King Philip and his little upstart, Alexander the Great. As if that wasn't enough', continued Demosthenes as his voice rose in anger, 'the Turks later occupied my sacred Greece and turned the Parthenon into a mosque. Soon the Turks went to war with the Venetians. The Venetians bombarded the Acropolis and the Parthenon because the Turks used the Acropolis as a stronghold and the Parthenon as an ammunition bunker.'

'Oh my', said Liz.

'Wow', said David. 'I can only imagine what happened next.'

---

[1] *Yiassas*: a toast meaning 'to your health'.

Demosthenes wiped the tears from his eyes. He then took a sip from his glass. 'Yes, *poulaki mou*, 1687 was not a very good year. The Parthenon, on whose steps I stood and spoke for hours in front of my countrymen, now stands like a run-down, abandoned commercial building in a slum. Oh how it breaks my heart!'

'Oh you poor, poor man', said Liz. 'If I only could help restore the Parthenon ... '

'You can't. But in spirit you have.' Demosthenes looked over at David. 'You have created a gifted, talented young man. With practice, he can become a great speaker, like myself and others who once mesmerized the masses with their eloquence.'

David placed his hands over his red face. 'I think this is ... '

'Oh my wonderful son.' His mother came over and hugged her son, kissed him on the forehead, and sat back in her chair.

'I think this is ... ' repeated David.

'But enough of me speaking', interrupted Demosthenes. 'It's time to let your young seed blossom into a great orator.' Demosthenes reached into his pocket and pulled out some pebbles and popped them into his mouth.

'Well, I hardly consider ... ' said David.

'Now you listen to what ... what ... Demost has to say, David', said Liz. 'He has your interests at heart.'

'Yes, mom.'

Demosthenes cleared his throat. 'It's appropriate that we discuss further details about rehearsal. Are you both ready?'

'Yes', said David.

Liz nodded her head.

'Excellent. Now there are still some basic but important ideas. If ... I mean ... after you've successfully given your presentation before the New Projects Council we'll discuss in more detail the Pebbles of Wisdom that you've learned, in the context of giving a presentation to explain and then persuade. That is ... '

'That is what?' David asked.

'That is if your presentation succeeds tomorrow.'

'It will', David said.

'That's the point. Positive thinking is necessary for giving an effective presentation. And that's exactly my first point. You have to think positive. You must reinforce that positive attitude in order to succeed. If you let your mind think about the negative, you'll have a negative result. It's like riding a horse. I remember riding my horse into battle ... '

'You were a soldier?'

'Yes. A general, in fact.'

'Oh my', said Liz. 'A general?'

'Yes, Liz, a general. Anyway, I rode my horse into battle. At first, I was nervous, even negative. And my horse sensed it. The animal bucked and even refused my orders. I then forced myself to think positively about riding the horse. The animal no longer sensed my nervousness and I was able to lead not only my horse but my men as well.'

'What a wonderful story', said Liz.

'And, Liz, I managed to survive even though we were defeated at Chaeronea and managed to deliver one of my best funeral orations.' Demosthenes raised his glass into the air. 'To Athens.'

Liz and David followed suit.

'The next thing to consider is to watch your time limit', said Demosthenes. 'Do not, I repeat, do not exceed your allotted time. When you rehearse, make sure that you fall within the time limit.'

'Why?' asked David.

'Because if other speakers follow, you eat up their time. It makes them feel you're belabouring them', continued the Greek, 'and that their time is not valuable. Besides, if you give a super presentation and finish under the allotted time, they'll ask ... no beg ... you to come back and give them more.'

'Let's see', said David. 'So far it's be positive and keep within the allotted time. What else?'

'You want to keep your mind focused on the purpose of the presentation', said Demosthenes. 'In this case, it's what?'

'To inform. To tell them what I want to do', said David.

'Good. And keep that in the forefront of your mind', said Demosthenes. 'That way you avoid digressing and you focus the audience's attention, too. And that leads on to the next point.'

'What's that?' asked Liz before David could utter a word.

'Yeah, what?' joined David.

'It's the audience.' Demosthenes pointed at David. 'Keep your audience in the forefront of your mind. Who they are and why they're there. You're presenting to them. No one else. The minute you forget about your audience you lose them.'

'That's wonderful advice', Liz said. 'Are you getting all this, son?'

'Yes, mom', said David. 'Anything else?'

'Yes, yes there is, in fact.' Demosthenes looked at Liz and winked.

David noticed that his mother blushed. 'What is it, Demost?'

'You have to work on polishing your delivery', said Demosthenes. 'You know, get rid of those distracting mannerisms.'

'Oh, like what?' asked Liz.

Demosthenes smiled and winked at Liz. 'You have none. But since you asked I'll mention a few that other people have. Like jingling change in their pockets. Playing with a pointer. Walking around and babbling like walkie-talkies.'

Liz chuckled.

David grew impatient. He wanted to start rehearsing, not listen to the Greek charm his mother. 'What's next?'

'Finally, for now anyway, you need to work on your voice. Not only do you want to speak clearly, but you also need to work on using your voice.'

'I see', said David. 'You mean manipulating my voice like a singer.'

'That's correct', said Demosthenes. He lowered his voice. 'Now I will let you both in on a secret.'

'Oh dear, what is it?' asked Liz.

'Yeah, what?'

Demosthenes spat pebbles into a water glass.

David watched as his mother grimaced. He couldn't help but smile.

'I had a terrible stammer', said the Greek. 'I was so bad that I couldn't say any word with an "r" in it and was called by all my friends and enemies, I might add, *batalos*. It means "the stammerer". I put pebbles in my mouth to control this affliction.'

'Oh, Demost', said Liz, placing her hand gently over her mouth. 'That's so sad yet so remarkable.'

'How?' asked David.

'Why David', said his mother, 'how could you be so insensitive? Here's a ... great man ... who had trouble speaking and became one of the greatest speakers of all time!'

'Thank you, Liz', said Demosthenes. 'You're very kind.'

'All right, all right', said David. 'I see. Okay, Demost. Are you finished so I can begin?'

'Not yet.'

'Then', said David, 'what's next?'

'You have just learned the next P. You must tell me what it is.'

'Let's see', said David as he rubbed his chin. 'We've covered Perspective ... Perception ... Planning ... Preparation ... hmmm ... a P, huh?'

'Yes', said Demosthenes. 'A P.'

'I think I know', said Liz. 'Can I say?'

'No, mom.' David snapped. 'Let me figure it out, myself.'

'Go ahead, Liz', disagreed Demosthenes. He said softly to her, 'One should never quiet a beautiful, intelligent woman.'

David crossed his arms.

'Oh my', said Liz. 'I think the P stands for Practice.'

'Brilliant', said Demosthenes. He raised his glass into the air. 'To Liz, the embodiment of Athena and Aphrodite.'

Liz blushed.

David held up his glass in the air and raised his voice. 'Now can I practise?'

'You may begin', said Demosthenes.

'Yes', agreed his mother. 'Demost says it's okay.'

# Chapter 22

David fell into his chair. 'Well, what do you two think?'

'I think you still need practice', said Demosthenes. 'But for the first presentation, you'll get by.'

'And you, mom?' David asked.

'Well, you're not like your father. But you've got potential.'

'With comments like that, it's going to be difficult to think positive', said David. He gulped the remaining ouzo in his glass.

'David, my young friend', said the Greek orator. 'You'll do fine. It takes more than one practice session, even several real presentations, to become an outstanding presenter. Besides, you'll do better once the nervous energy rises to the surface and you direct it into your presentation.'

'He's right, you know', said Liz.

David wanted to say to his mother that she was sounding more and more like a parrot but didn't want to upset her.

'Besides', said Demosthenes, 'I'll watch you give your presentation. We'll build on that experience and prepare for the next one before the Executive Steering Committee.'

'Huh? How?' David asked. 'There's no visitors. Just me.'

'I'll be there', said Demosthenes. 'I'll manage to hang around somehow.'

He looked at his watch. 'I prefer sundials. But for now this digital timepiece will do. It's getting late. I must go now and you need your rest, David.' He turned towards Liz. 'I was charmed by your company and your food. So, like Hermes, god of speed and Zeus's messenger, I must leave. But before I do, David, I must give you something.'

Demosthenes pulled from his frock a small string of black pebbles. He handed it to David as he rose from the table and headed for the door. 'Those are called *komboloia*.[1] You hold them when you get nervous and as you play with them your worries will disappear. It should help you relax tonight.'

David watched as the Greek waltzed over to his mother, took a bow, and kissed her on the hand.

'Good night, Aphrodite. Until next time … ' He then walked towards the door to the apartment and closed it behind him, leaving Liz stunned and David playing with his worry beads.

---

[1] *Komboloia*: worry beads.

# Chapter 23

The shapely secretary led David to the large mahogany doors. He watched as she took hold of the huge brass handles and eased the doors apart.

His heart pounded. His hands grew moist. His breathing accelerated. Darn it, he thought, I forgot my worry beads.

'Mr Michaels is here to give his presentation on the Brazilian project', said the secretary, leading him to the dais where five people sat. Behind them was a large plate glass window revealing the skyline of the city.

All five people rose from their chairs and extended their hands. They quickly exchanged introductions.

'Please take the podium', said the chairwoman, pointing to a large mahogany piece of furniture. Beside it was an overhead projector and behind that a white screen.

Demost, where are you? he thought. You said you'd be here.

'You may begin', said the chairwoman.

David crept up to the podium. He positioned his material and inspected the projector. As he directed his attention to the audience he saw something that nobody would believe even if he told them. Saddled in a rope seat on the other side of the window was the Greek orator, Demosthenes. Hanging from his ears was a stethoscope with the diaphragm pressed again the glass.

David then remembered what Demosthenes told him about nervous energy. He had to direct it into his presentation. A surge of energy overcame him, unlike anything he had ever experienced before an audience, especially after Demosthenes gave a wave of the hand.

'Members of the New Projects Council, I would like to tell you about an idea of mine. It's called Love is for Everyone – or LIFE for short.'

He briefly noticed the eyes staring at him. David picked up copies of the presentation and handed them to his listeners. He returned to the podium and switched on the overhead projector. The agenda appeared.

---

### YUGGENHEIM FOUNDATION

### LOVE IS FOR EVERYONE PROPOSAL

---

**Love is for Everyone Proposal**

**David Michaels**

**October 27, 19XX**

---

# YUGGENHEIM FOUNDATION

## LOVE IS FOR EVERYONE PROPOSAL

## AGENDA

☞ **Introduction**

☞ **Background**

☞ **Proposal**

☞ **Benefits**

☞ **Requirements**

☞ **Conclusion**

☞ **Next Steps**

'Ladies and gentlemen', he continued. 'I shall first give a brief introduction and background ... ' He noticed that they were paying more attention to the handouts than to himself. He also noticed that Demosthenes was shaking his head as he jotted notes in a small booklet.

' ... From there I shall present my proposal, describe the benefits, and the requirements for making it a reality. I shall then summarize my main points and offer some ideas on what the next steps are.'

'Can we ask questions during the presentation or afterwards?' asked a woman listener, raising her head.

David looked at the window. He watched Demosthenes continue to scribble. 'I prefer after the presentation.'

'Please continue', said the woman.

'Yes', said another council member, 'Do.'

'Ah ... yeah ... sure.' David struggled for a second to regain his composure. He showed the next slide on the screen.

## YUGGENHEIM FOUNDATION

## LOVE IS FOR EVERYONE PROPOSAL

### INTRODUCTION

### PURPOSE

**Set up hospital facility site and hospital ship to traverse the Amazon Basin**

'Ah ... the purpose of this presentation is to inform you of my desire to ... ' He looked up at the slide and began to read verbatim: ' ... set up a hospital facility site and hospital ship to traverse the Amazon Basin. As you can see', continued David, now standing between the projector and the screen, thereby partially projecting his silhouette on the latter, 'the Amazon stretches for approximately four thousand miles in South America.'

David noticed the listeners moving their heads to try to see the map. He looked up at Demosthenes, noticing the Greek waving his arms. David took the cue and moved back behind the podium.

He paused for a few seconds and then switched slides.

---

### YUGGENHEIM FOUNDATION

### LOVE IS FOR EVERYONE PROPOSAL

---

### INTRODUCTION

### SCOPE

Provide healthcare
services to at-risk
and underprivileged
children

---

He started to read but a glimpse at Demost took him aback. The Greek was shaking his head. David knew right away what Demosthenes meant. He placed his notes aside on the podium, looked at the audience squarely in the eyes and continued. 'This entails offering badly needed healthcare services to poor and other less than fortunate children throughout the Amazon Basin.

'But before I go into … ah … more details', said David as he changed to the next slide, 'I want to give you some background information.

## YUGGENHEIM FOUNDATION

## LOVE IS FOR EVERYONE PROPOSAL

### BACKGROUND

Yuggenheim Foundation

☞ Supports charitable causes

☞ Cares about saving our planet and its inhabitants

☞ Interested in commodities in South America

Yuggenheim Headquarters, International

'The Yuggenheim Foundation ... you know ... the very Foundation that we have all been involved in for a long time, is known to support charitable causes. This entails caring about saving our planet and its inhabitants. It also entails expressing an interest in commodities in South America.' He started feeling more comfortable and loosened his grip on the podium. He looked at Demosthenes who pointed his thumb towards the sky. David became more positive and switched to the next slide.

**YUGGENHEIM FOUNDATION**

**LOVE IS FOR EVERYONE PROPOSAL**

**PROPOSAL**

Build and deploy
hospital facility site

Acquire and deploy
hospital ship

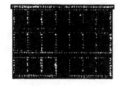

He noticed that he was still vying for the attention of the listeners. Most were still looking at the handout. 'Now ... you know
... I can go into more detail about the purpose of the presentation. My proposal really consists of ... ah ... two parts. You
know, one, I propose we build and deploy a hospital facility site.
I'd like ... ah ... to elaborate on this.'

He noticed their heads were gradually looking at him. He also
saw Demosthenes waving his finger. David stood just right of the
podium, moved towards the audience and continued to speak as
Demosthenes nodded his head and shoved his thumb skyward.
Now David had everyone's attention.

107

'Basically, it means … ah … four key considerations.' David stuck a finger into the air. 'One, it means employing modern equipment and technology.' He stuck up another finger. 'Two, hire a professional staff.' Another finger went up. 'Three, ensure sufficient medical supplies are available.' A fourth finger went up. 'Four, provide adequate space for patients.'

He pointed to the second item. 'The other part of the proposal means acquiring and deploying a hospital ship. Like building and deploying a hospital facility site, it too requires the same four considerations.'

He returned to the podium and changed slides.

---

**YUGGENHEIM FOUNDATION**

**LOVE IS FOR EVERYONE PROPOSAL**

---

### BENEFITS

Yuggenheim Foundation

☞ Publicized worldwide
humanitarian statement

☞ Better understanding of
Brazilian commodities

☞ Improved market penetration
of products and services

☞ Opportunity for tax benefits

---

'You know', he continued, 'there are many benefits for the Yuggenheim Foundation.' David removed a pointer from his chest pocket, extended it and pointed to the first item with his back turned towards the audience. 'It will tell the world that the Foundation cares about humanity. It will give the Foundation a better understanding of Brazilian commodities. Ah ... it will enable a much improved penetration of the Yuggenheim

Corporation's products and services. Finally, it will provide the Corporation … you know … with an opportunity for greater tax benefits.'

David turned towards the audience and played with the pointer as he spoke and switched to the next slide.

---

### YUGGENHEIM FOUNDATION

### LOVE IS FOR EVERYONE PROPOSAL

---

**BENEFITS**

Brazilian Government

☞ Improved healthcare to millions of children

☞ Economy boost

☞ Venture opportunity with foreign private corporation

---

'The country of … ah … Brazil will receive several benefits.' He extended the pointer and momentarily looked at Demosthenes as he turned. The Greek waved his finger in a circular motion.

David recognized what the Greek signalled. He positioned himself to the side of the screen, making sure he faced the audience, and pointed to the first item. 'Millions of children in the ... ah ... Amazon Basin, you know, will receive better healthcare.' He pointed to the second item, being careful to face the audience. 'The Brazilians get a spark to their economy.' He moved down to the third and final item. 'Finally ... ah ... the Brazilians have the chance to join up with a successful foreign corporation.'

He dropped the pointer to his side and returned to the podium. As he spoke, he played with the pointer by opening and closing it. 'In the end ... you know ... everyone benefits.' He saw Demosthenes repeatedly moving his hands together and apart. David looked at his hands and closed the pointer one last time and put it into his shirt pocket. He removed the slide and put another in its place.

```
┌─────────────────────────────────────────────────┐
│                                                   │
│           YUGGENHEIM FOUNDATION                   │
│                                                   │
│                                                   │
│         LOVE IS FOR EVERYONE PROPOSAL             │
│                                                   │
├─────────────────────────────────────────────────┤
│                                                   │
│                 REQUIREMENTS                      │
│                                                   │
│                                                   │
│      ☞    Assign programme manager                │
│                                                   │
│      ☞    Allocate funding                        │
│                                                   │
│                                                   │
│                                                   │
│                                                   │
│                                                   │
└─────────────────────────────────────────────────┘
```

'Realizing these benefits, you know, involves fulfilling two requirements. First, to appoint a programme manager. Second, to allocate funding for both, you know, the hospital facility site and the hospital ship.' He noticed that the Greek pointed at his watch; David glanced at his own, recognizing that only three minutes remained. He switched slides.

```
┌─────────────────────────────────────────────────┐
│                                                   │
│          YUGGENHEIM FOUNDATION                    │
│                                                   │
│                                                   │
│       LOVE IS FOR EVERYONE PROPOSAL               │
│                                                   │
├───────────────────────────────────────────────────┤
│                                                   │
│                  CONCLUSION                       │
│                                                   │
│                                                   │
│      ☞   Project has positive payback             │
│                                                   │
│      ☞   Project has global impact                │
│                                                   │
│                                                   │
│                                                   │
│                                                   │
│                                                   │
└─────────────────────────────────────────────────┘
```

'So you can see, the LIFE proposal offers good payback, both financially and in intangible ways. But it ... ah ... also has global impact by helping unfortunate children and, consequently, promotes goodness in the world.' He looked at his watch.

He changed the slide.

```
┌─────────────────────────────────────────┐
│                                           │
│        YUGGENHEIM FOUNDATION              │
│                                           │
│                                           │
│     LOVE IS FOR EVERYONE PROPOSAL         │
│                                           │
├───────────────────────────────────────────┤
│                                           │
│              NEXT STEPS                   │
│                                           │
│                                           │
│   ☞   Approval from New Projects          │
│       Council                             │
│                                           │
│   ☞   Explanatory presentation to         │
│       Executive Steering Committee         │
│                                           │
│                                           │
│                                           │
│                                           │
└─────────────────────────────────────────┘
```

'So where do we go from here? There are two essential steps. One, I need approval from you, you know, the New Projects Council. And two, I then proceed to give an explanatory presentation to the Executive Steering Committee.'

David pulled the slide from the overhead projector but failed to turn the machine off. 'Are there any questions?'

David noticed Demosthenes signalling him to turn something off but he couldn't work it out. He looked at his watch but the time indicated that one minute remained. He watched as the listeners scrambled through their copies of his presentation.

Maybe I went on too long, he thought. He remembered that it was better to finish early rather than late. 'Thank you for this ... ah ... you know, opportunity.' He picked up the slides and notes and headed towards the double doors.

'Wait a second, Mr Michaels', said one of the listeners. 'Please.'

David turned and looked at the man who gave the polite but formal order. He also noticed Demosthenes raising his hands towards the sky as a sign of forgiveness or frustration. 'Yes sir?'

'Are there any other similar humanitarian efforts going on in Brazil?'

David froze in his tracks. A lump came to his throat as a response came to his lips. He replied in a high pitch: 'Yes ... no ... '

The listeners turned and looked at each other; some of them shook their heads while others had a smirk on their faces.

'Thank you for listening and thank you for your time', said David as he continued for the door.

'We will let you know tomorrow by eight-thirty in the morning of our decision', said the chairwoman.

David noticed that the Greek was no longer hanging around; he was ready to do the same.

# Chapter 24

David wove his way through the crowded city streets. It was certainly a lot different being within the crowd, David thought, than in front of it. All you had to do was blend in; you didn't have a bunch of eyes staring at you, waiting for you to fail. Thank God it's over. That was the most emotionally draining moment of my life.

As he turned the corner, he felt a dull but noticeable ping on the back of his neck. 'What was that?' He turned.

He froze in his tracks as he looked down at his feet and noticed a moist pebble. He looked up and saw Demosthenes.

'Demost!' said David. 'That was very clever of you to hang outside the window and listen with a stethoscope. Real sleuth-like. Should have been a stunt man in Hollywood. Or at least a special effects man.'

Demosthenes took a bow. 'Why thank you, *poulaki mou*. But all speakers are stunt men and special effects men.'

'You can say that again', said David. 'Well, I suppose you're following me because you're ready to criticize me for the way I gave my presentation.'

Demosthenes looked round. Then he placed his arm around David's shoulders and said, 'Let's not talk here. As we used to say in Greece, "King Philip's ears and eyes are everywhere." Follow me.'

David followed the orator into a small coffee shop.

'Let's talk here.' They followed the waitress to a corner booth. Both sat as she poured them coffee. 'In ancient Greece discussing problems in a coffee house, called a *kafenion*, seemed always to soothe one's nerves. So tell me, *poulaki mou*, how do you feel?'

David took a gulp of his coffee. 'Relieved. I'm glad it's over. But I'm not too proud of my performance.'

'Nonsense', said Demosthenes. 'You did fine.'

'I did?'

'Sure. What you're feeling now is what even the very best presenters feel. Why, I felt that way after I gave my first Philippic.'

'You did?'

'It's true. I was so energetic going in that afterwards I felt emotionally and physically drained. All I said to myself was that this was the worst experience of my life and that it was a failure.'

'You felt that way, too?'

'You bet', said Demosthenes. 'The key is to learn from your experience so that the next performance gets even better. It's like what you call today, buyer's remorse. You get the product and afterwards you're filled with regret, sorrow, even disappointment, especially in yourself because your fears take over.'

'Yeah', said David. 'That's just as I feel. I guess you can say I have speaker's remorse.'

Demosthenes chuckled. 'Very good, *poulaki mou*. I'll have to remember that.' Demosthenes spat a pebble into an ashtray. 'It's time to discuss your presentation. First, let's discuss what went right.'

'Okay', said David, followed by a deep breath. 'Okay.'

'The presentation was very logical. Had good supporting detail. And you appeared very sincere.'

'What you're saying is that I had good *logos*, *pathos* and *ethos*', said David, proudly.

'Exactly.' Demosthenes winked. 'That's a sign of good preparation.'

'But what about my delivery?'

'Well, you had good voice projection. I was even able to hear you without the stethoscope, though faintly.'

'Anything else?'

'You appeared to control your nervousness even though I venture to guess you were very nervous.'

'You bet I was', said David. 'Scared stiff!'

'You seemed for the most part to have an understanding of the six Ps. You know ... '

'Perspective. Perception. Planning. Preparation. Practice ... '

'Exactly. But you should have learned the last P. What is it?'

David took a sip of coffee. 'Let's see, it begins with P ... hm ... I think it must be Performance.'

'That's right. Not bad for the first try. It's a tough one to experience let alone guess what it is.' Demosthenes spat another pebble into the ashtray. 'Your presentation was very good for perspective, perception, planning and preparation. But ... '

'But what?' asked David. His heart raced, for now he could sense the hard part of the conversation coming.

'It was quite clear that you needed more practice to perfect your performance.'

'But I practised once last night.'

'One practice session is not enough', said Demosthenes. 'And practising under the influence of ouzo doesn't exactly help in improving your delivery. Let me tell you what I did. Sometimes for days I would hide myself in a cave and practise. I wouldn't leave until I had perfected my delivery. To make sure that I wouldn't leave until I felt I had perfected everything I shaved only half my face. That way, I stayed in the cave because I didn't want anybody

118

to see me that way. But you don't have to take such extreme measures. You just need to practise more. I got carried away.'

'So how many times should you practise?' David asked, crossing his arms.

'Three separate sessions is normal but that's a guideline, not a rule. But enough of that. Let's talk about your delivery so that you can practise avoiding the same mistakes when performing before the Executive Steering Committee.'

'You mean *if* I perform in front of the Executive Steering Committee.'

'We'll see. I put in a good word to Zeus for you.'

'Thanks', said David, tightening his arms across his chest.

'Let's take each item in turn', said Demosthenes as he removed a small notebook and read from a list. 'I must say that you made two big errors right away.'

'And what were they?' asked David, sharply.

'Don't be defensive. A fiery look is coming over your face. The same look that Ares, the god of war, had before going into battle.'

'Sorry', said David. He took a deep breath. 'Go ahead.'

'One, if you have handouts distribute them after the presentation, not before or during. You don't want the audience to redirect their concentration from you to the handout.'

'Yeah, I noticed that. It really bugged me.' David lowered his arms. 'You're right.'

'It's best to distribute handouts towards the end of your presentation unless, of course, some people can't see the slides. Then you really have no choice but to distribute them to the audience at the start.' Demosthenes took a sip of coffee. 'Now for big mistake number two.'

'And what's that?' David asked.

'You didn't indicate whether the audience could ask questions, and, if so, when.'

'Yeah', said David with a sigh. 'I remember that too. It caused some confusion.'

'You need to tell the audience when they can ask questions. It eliminates confusion. And, by the way, you need to work on handling questions.'

'Yeah, that one question caught me off guard.' David took a sip. 'I don't handle questions very well.'

'I know', agreed Demosthenes. 'At another time and place we'll discuss the fine art of handling questions. For now, let's discuss your delivery.'

David nodded.

'Here it was clear that you needed to practise more to improve your performance. Your lack of practice may very well have influenced the New Projects Council's decision whether or not to proceed.'

'Why? Because I made a few mistakes?'

'David, let me impart another bit of unsolicited advice by using the analogy of a smorgasbord.'

'A what?'

'A smorgasbord. A buffet. You have these nowadays, don't you?'

'Yeah sure, but ... '

'Just listen', said Demosthenes. 'In a smorgasbord, appearance means a lot. Everything must not only be prepared perfectly but must appear perfect. If the food tastes fine but does not look appetizing, few people will partake of its delights.'

'So', said David, 'people judge a book by its cover. Is that what you're saying?'

'Sort of, but there's also a need for some substance between the covers.'

'I see.' David took a sip. 'Okay, tell me what you saw. I don't see how I can hurt any more than I do. You know, the wound can't be any deeper.'

'You took the words right out of my mouth.'

'Ah ... '

'There you go again, David. You took more words out of my mouth.'

'I don't understand.' David raised his shoulders as a perplexed look covered his countenance.

'Ah, you know', said Demosthenes with a smile, 'you understand more than you really give yourself credit for.'

'Oh? How so?' David crossed his arms.

'Well, for one, you used "Ah" too many times.'

'I did?'

Demosthenes nodded. 'You also kept saying "You know" quite a few times, too.'

'Yeah, you're right. I did. I guess it did sound a little stupid.'

Demosthenes raised an index finger into the air. 'Not stupid. Only unrehearsed. Through practice you can overcome that habit.'

'What else?' David eased his arms down.

'Let's discuss the use of the pointer. Quite frankly, you sometimes played with that contraption as if it were an accordion rather than a tool to pinpoint information on the slide.'

'I was nervous', said David. 'All right, I admit it was a distraction. But it made me feel more comfortable because I had something to hold on to.'

'Speaking of holding on to something', said the Greek orator, 'you held on to that podium sometimes like a cat hanging from a telephone pole. Your knuckles were turning white.'

David could feel the blood rush to his head as a sense of embarrassment overcame him. 'As I said, I was nervous.'

'Also related to the last point is that you remained too stationary. You needed to move around more. You reminded me of a victim of Medusa. It was as if, at times, you saw her and were turned to stone.'

'Sorry', said David.

'No apology required. It just takes experience and practice. Now for the next point, and it deals with slides.'

121

'Slides?'

'Slides', repeated Demosthenes. 'First, never talk to the slides. You turned your back to the audience and talked. Rude. Very rude.'

'I didn't mean it.'

'True. But how do they know? Besides the interaction is with the audience, not with the slide. The slide doesn't listen.'

'Next.'

'Don't be defensive, David. I know this hurts. But it's for your own good.' Demosthenes sipped his coffee. 'Now remember, never block the image on the screen.'

'I did that?'

'Yes, *poulaki mou*, you did. That just frustrates listeners, especially if the image requires them to see the slide. Keep your silhouette out of the picture. You're not that great modern version of the dramatist Sophocles, Alfred Hitchcock. Though I must admit, you're a lot thinner and have more hair than he had.'

'Anything else about my use of slides?'

'Why yes, David, there is.' Demosthenes spat a pebble into the ashtray. 'Never read verbatim anything on a slide. It's boring and insults the intelligence of your listeners. They can read as easily as you can. Besides, if they can't read it then the type is too small and if they can, why do they need you?'

'Good point. Didn't realize I was reading the slide.' David sighed. 'That's it?'

'No, *poulaki mou*. That's not it. One last thing about slides. Never let the overhead projector shoot a blank image on the screen while you continue to talk.'

'Then what should I do?'

'Turn off the projector. Make your point without it. The bright, blank light and the hum of the machine only distracts people from what you're saying. If you need to use the projector later, wait for that time and turn the machine back on. The audience isn't there to see bright lights or listen to the hum of an overhead projector. They're there to listen and watch you and receive your message.'

A short silence ensued. David stared into his cup. 'Any more?'

'Your cup's not empty yet', Demosthenes said. 'You still have a little left.'

'Go ahead.'

'Just one more point. You never, repeat never, thank the audience when you've given a presentation. They expressed an interest in what you have to say and want you to say it. It is they who should thank you.'

'I guess', said David, 'I shouldn't bother to thank you.'

'For what?'

'For paying the bill for the coffee', said David, rising from the table.

# Chapter 25

It was a restless night for David. He tossed and turned in bed. His head ached. His stomach felt sour. Four times during the night he got up and paced around the study room and stared at the papers taped to the walls. If only I had practised more, he thought.

He entered the kitchen; his mother was not yet up. He poured himself a bowl of cereal and a cup of coffee. He looked at his watch: eight-twenty. He turned on the small colour television on the counter.

The morning news flashed across the screen. As he listened and watched, he noticed a famous political figure facing a hostile crowd. Someone in the audience had mocked what the politician said and another yelled obscenities that were masked by the television station with a series of beeps. Even in the midst of such rejection David noticed that the politician continued to speak and stay calm. Thank God, he thought, I didn't have that type of reception. Then again, I might experience a reception like that over the phone.

'There's my brave son', said his mother as she walked into the kitchen. 'I didn't hear you come in last night.'

'I was with Demost.'

'What a lovely man. Did he help you like he promised?'

'More than you could imagine', said David. 'I guess you can say he hung around for the entire show.'

'So how did your presentation go?'

David choked on his cereal. He was able to speak again after washing down the food with his coffee. 'Fine. My delivery wasn't great. It may have hurt my chances. I'll know better in about five minutes.'

'Five minutes? Why five minutes?'

'That's when they'll let me know whether I can proceed to the Executive Steering Committee and explain how to deploy my proposal.'

'What does Demost think?' asked Liz.

'As I told you, he said my delivery needed help but he thought it went fine. But I'm not so sure.'

The phone rang.

David pushed himself away from the table. He pressed the receiver against his ear. 'Michaels' residence.'

'Mr Michaels?' a female voice asked.

'Yes.' His head pounded. His hands and forehead became wet. All the symptoms of standing before an audience.

'This is Gloria Reinman of the Yuggenheim Foundation.'

'Yes, yes', he said. Skip the preliminaries, baby, he thought.

'This call is about your presentation before the New Projects Council.'

'Yes.' Come on, lady, he thought, get to the point.

'The Council would like you to proceed to the next step.'

'Yes. Yes!'

'That would be … '

'Giving a presentation before the Executive Steering Committee?'

'Why yes, Mr Michaels.'

125

'Yahoo!' screamed David as he placed his hand over the receiver. He then removed his hand. 'Tell me something.'

'Yes, Mr Michaels?'

'Could you tell me how the council voted?' asked David. 'You know, the split?'

'Certainly. Just one moment as I look it up in the minutes.'

David winked at his mother. She came over and gave him a hug.

'Mr Michaels?'

'Yes.'

'The vote was a close one. Three to two in your favour.'

'Were there any comments?'

'Yes, there were some ... Let's see ... they felt that in general you gave a good presentation although your delivery needed improvement.'

'Anything else?'

'They believed that you didn't answer their questions very well and that more detail would be necessary for the Executive Steering Committee. They also noted that if the proposal goes to the Board of Directors for final approval it will be difficult to sell. By the way, Mr Michaels, the presentation before the Executive Steering Committee is scheduled to be in two days, this Friday, same room, at nine in the morning.'

'Thank you very much', said David, hanging up the receiver. He turned towards his mother. 'Well, mom, I did it.'

'I'm proud of you, son. You should call Demost right away to let him know the results. Or should I?'

# Chapter 26

'Congratulations, *poulaki mou.*' Demosthenes clapped his hands. In a second or two, Demetri scurried over to the table in the lounge. 'Demetri, fill two glasses of wine and bring them to us.' He turned towards David. 'This is indeed a big moment for us.'

Demetri disappeared.

'Demost', said David. 'I owe you a lot.'

'You owe me not one drachma, *poulaki mou.*'

'No', persisted David. 'It's true. If I hadn't learned the six Pebbles of Wisdom, it would have turned out a disaster.'

Demetri served the wine. He also put the bottle and *mezedakia*[1] on the table and departed.

'Cheers', said Demosthenes, raising his glass.

David followed suit, and said, 'Cheers to the greatest orator and Greek of all time.' He noticed Demosthenes blushing.

'You do me a great honour, David.'

---

[1]*Mezedakia*: appetizer of cheeses, breads, olives, lamb and fish.

'You deserve every bit. Now I have to give a presentation before the Executive Steering Committee.' David began to taste the *mezedakia*.

'And what type of a presentation might that be?'

'One that explains how I'm going to accomplish what I want to do. The lady on the telephone said this one will be tougher. The vote by the New Projects Council was a close call.'

'Let's see', said Demosthenes as he popped some pebbles into his mouth. 'An explanatory presentation ... '

'That's right. An explanatory presentation.'

'Now remember, *poulaki mou*, everything I have told you still applies. The six Ps still apply. They are all relevant.'

'Great. I'll get started right away. I have two days before the presentation.'

'Two days? That doesn't give us much time.'

David downed his wine and started to rise.

'Wait a second', said Demosthenes. 'Not so fast. There's more to learn about presentations in general and giving explanatory presentations in particular.'

'There is?' said David, falling back into his chair.

'There most certainly is, *poulaki mou*. There most certainly is.' The Greek rose from the table and walked on to the stage. From behind the curtain, he pulled the flipchart stand that had become so familiar to David. 'Let's talk a bit about your explanatory presentation, incorporating some of the ideas you learned previously and learning new ones.' He wrote 'Perspective' at the top of the page.

'Right, perspective. So?'

Demosthenes spat a pebble into the spittoon at the base of the flipchart stand.

'Tell me about the audience you'll be addressing.'

'Well, let's see ... hm ... it consists of seven people', observed David.

Demosthenes scribbled on the flipchart. 'What else?'

'The committee consists of more senior executives.'

The Greek scribbled.

'I assume that the committee will make a decision that will maximize gain and minimize pain for everyone involved. The Corporation. The Foundation. The children being helped by the project. It will, therefore, pass judgment on my proposal and forward its remarks to the Board of Directors.'

'Anything else?' asked Demosthenes. 'What can you determine about their backgrounds?'

'I've no idea. But I'm sure the members of the committee are more experienced and are a fairly intelligent lot.'

Demosthenes wrote the last note. 'So what can we deduce from this information?'

'Well ... ' David scratched his face. 'I'd say that since they are higher-level managers they will have less need of detailed information but demand more of the right information to make a good decision.'

'Excellent.' Demosthenes then flipped to a new page. He wrote 'Perception' at the top. 'Now let's discuss the next POW – first your perception of them.'

'Okay.' David took a sip of wine from his glass. 'My perception is that they're a group of executives ... '

Demosthenes wrote as David spoke.

' ... who are more interested in how I'm going to accomplish what I want to do', continued David, 'but at a higher level than the council.'

'KISS.'

'Huh?'

'KISS', repeated Demosthenes. 'It stands for *Keep It Short and Simple*. You don't want to make your presentation complicated.'

'Oh, I see. They perceive their time as important and their interests at a more, I suppose, strategic level.'

'Very good. Now then, let's discuss their perception of you.'

'Of me?' asked David, pointing to himself. 'Well, I guess they look at me as another former insider of the Corporation, trying to get money for a project. Perhaps a little young. But nonetheless having a solid track record with the Yuggenheim Corporation.'

Demosthenes wrote.

'I also think they view me as an expert in what I choose to do. I mean as an expert in managing projects, not necessarily in the healing arts.' David stroked his face. 'That means I'd better appear to have good plans on how I expect to complete the project ... '

'Speaking of planning,' interrupted Demosthenes, 'let's discuss that topic next.' He flipped the page and wrote 'Planning' at the top. 'All the same principles of planning apply as in your presentation to the New Projects Council.'

'You mean create a good logical outline, you know, *logos*.'

'That's right', scribbled Demosthenes. 'And?'

'Adding detail in a way that emotionally involves the audience so it will support me. You know, *pathos*.'

'Yes. Yes. Go on.'

David gave a wide smile as he watched the Greek scribble away. 'And *ethos* to reflect your credibility and veracity with the audience.'

'Credibility and veracity? Big words', said Demosthenes, 'for being truthful. I like them.'

'A thesaurus can be helpful.' David scratched his head. 'Back to *logos*. I guess I can retain some of the basic structure. No?'

'Sure. But don't make it the same rehash of the last presentation. The purposes are different and so is the audience.' Demosthenes flipped to a new, blank sheet of paper. 'What's next?'

'Let's see. I know', said David snapping his fingers, 'preparation.'

'Perfect', said the Greek, scribbling. 'Now here's where some of the biggest changes will be required.'

'I know one of them. I will present less of what I presented earlier because the Executive Steering Committee will get a preview from the New Projects Council.'

'Good.'

'But', said David, 'there will be another change.'

'How's that?' asked Demosthenes, scribbling.

'The committee will want to know more of how I plan to do what I want to do but with the minimum of details.'

'Very good.' Demosthenes spat a pebble into the spittoon. 'Now I think, *poulaki mou*, it's time to discuss the use of illustrations in a presentation.'

'Illustrations?'

'Diagrams, charts, maps, pictures. The whole gambit.' Demosthenes flipped to a new page. 'Remember what Confucius said ... '

'Yeah, I know. A picture's worth a thousand words. But I've already used a map.'

'That was good. But you need more illustrations, better ones to explain what you plan to implement. Remember, that's the focus of your presentation.'

David nodded. 'Okay, you win.' He took a sip from his glass. 'Talk.'

'No, it's not for me to talk. It's for you to listen.'

'Touché', said David. 'Okay, I'm listening.'

'Good. Now illustrations offer many benefits. Name some of them.'

'Well, they provide a lot of information on one page', said David.

'That's one', Demosthenes said, writing.

'They're easier to communicate with.'

'That's another.'

'They hold the reader's attention more.'

'Keep going', said Demosthenes.

'I'd also say that the committee will retain more of what you present because the image is burned in their minds.'

'Excellent.' Demosthenes flipped to a new page. 'I'd like to talk a little more about that last point.' He drew a diagram.

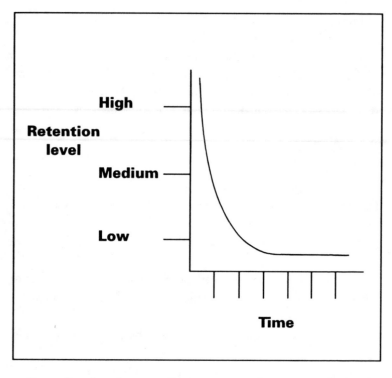

'Basically, this diagram illustrates just what you said. On the vertical axis is a continuum reflecting retention level. On the horizontal axis is a continuum reflecting time. Essentially, at the start of the presentation the retention factor of the audience is high. But as time progresses the retention level of the audience declines.

'But through illustrations, you can "burn" your information in their minds more easily and, consequently, their retention increases.'

'Wow!' said David. 'I'll never forget that.'

'Cute', said Demosthenes. 'Now to realize all of the above benefits, you need to keep some of the following points in mind.'

'Like what?' David felt his adrenaline running.

'Remember the points I made earlier about using illustrations?'

'You mean like being manageable ... relevant ... easy to use ... understandable ... clean ... clear ... ?'

'Very good, *poulaki mou*. I see that you do. But now I want to go into more detail about how to put together effective presentations that reflect those qualities.'

'Sounds good to me', said David as he watched the Greek flip to a new page and spit a pebble into the spittoon.

'The first point I'd like to make', said Demosthenes, 'is that an illustration should be designed for understandability and readability.' He spat a pebble into the spittoon. 'How do you do that?'

David ran his fingers through his hair. 'I guess one way is to have a title with the illustration.'

Demosthenes scribbled. 'What about some characteristics of the title?'

'It should be short but meaningful enough to describe what the illustration is about.'

'Excellent', said Demosthenes, writing. 'The title should cover the topic addressed but not seem like a title for a dissertation. Good. What else? Here's a clue: flow.'

'Flow? Well, I'd say that it should have a logical flow.'

'Good. What are ways to reflect this flow?'

David drummed his fingers on the table. 'I can display the information top–down ... bottom–up ... left to right ... spatially ... chronologically ... by relatedness ... '

'You've got the idea', said the Greek, scribbling, 'which is that there must be some logical sequence to what's shown in the illustration. That it's not just a hodgepodge of graphics to impress.'

'Nothing's worse than an illustration filled with garbage that makes you more confused than no picture.'

'Unless', said Demosthenes with a smirk, 'that's exactly what you want to do, confuse the listeners. But enough of that topic, *poulaki mou*. What else can you do to enhance understandability and readability?'

'I would ensure that there's plenty of white space in the illustration.'

'Why?'

'To help reduce the busyness of the illustration and improve receptivity of the material being shown', David said.

'Excellent.' Demosthenes wrote numbers on the paper. 'Here's a little heuristic, or rule of thumb, for illustrations. It will especially help with the white space problem.' He reached into his shirt pocket, removed a handful of pebbles and popped them into his mouth. 'Apply the seven plus two rule.'

'The what?'

'The seven plus two rule', repeated Demosthenes. 'It means that you should never have an illustration with more than nine objects on it – that's the sum of seven plus two. If there's more than nine objects, the human mind will have difficulty in understanding the illustration. Ideally, you want seven. The reason is that psychological tests have shown that the human mind can handle seven items of information at any point in time. Nine is about the upper limit after which the mind becomes overloaded. Remember, I mentioned that earlier.'

'Oh yeah. You did say something earlier about not exceeding nine items', said David. 'I like that. The rule of seven plus two.'

'KISS', said Demosthenes.

'KISS', retorted David, smiling. 'That is a good rule for keeping illustrations understandable for the audience. Good stuff.'

'Now let's talk about some more good stuff. Like print size.'

'Yeah', said David. 'That's a good one, too. I've been to presentations where the contents of an illustration required having the eyes of an eagle to read the information. Or a pair of binoculars.'

'It gets pretty hard to read such illustrations, doesn't it?'

'Sure does', said David.

'Not only does it make it difficult for the audience to see the contents, it makes it just as difficult for your listeners to concentrate on what you're saying. They're so busy trying to see that they can't listen.'

'I see what you're saying', said David. 'I mean I hear what you're saying.'

'Very witty, *poulaki mou*. Now let's discuss colour.'

'Colour?' David asked.

'That's right. Colour. First, let's discuss darkness of print. The characters in an illustration must be dark enough that members of the audience can read it, especially with slides.'

'Good point', said David. 'I've seen slides projected on a screen where everyone has had to struggle to read the print. Not that the print's too small, mind you, but because the ink on the slide is too light or too dark, thereby making it difficult to distinguish between characters, numbers or symbols.'

'There's another aspect to colour. Only this time it doesn't have to do with readability but rather impact.'

'Impact?' asked David.

'Yes, impact.' Demosthenes spat a pebble into the spittoon as he wrote. 'Some people overload illustrations with colour. They place colours in an illustration indiscriminately. The result is something akin to an artist's palette rather than an image to communicate a point.'

'So what you're really saying, Demost, is that the issue is not whether to use colour but if you choose to, use it wisely and sparingly.'

'Yes, *poulaki mou*. An illustration should use colours only if a purpose is served.'

'So mixing a bunch of red, green, yellow, blue, orange and the like', said David, 'may make the illustration pretty but may not necessarily communicate your point very well.'

'Couldn't have said it better myself', said Demosthenes. 'Now remember, certain colours have a psychological effect. Red indicates something negative. Green something positive. Yellow something cheerful. Whatever colour you employ, use it consistently.'

'I see', said David. 'That makes sense. I've seen presentations where the illustrations were so crowded with colours that I thought I was on the verge of blindness. It did take my concentration away from the presenter.'

'Now', said the Greek as he spat a pebble, 'I have one more point about illustrations.'

'That is … ?'

'That illustrations should not be used to alter the facts.'

'I don't understand', said David with a perplexed look on his face.

'In a way, you do. I'm talking about *ethos*. I am especially talking about statistical charts. You see, *poulaki mou*, some people draw charts that give a false impression that the facts are better or worse than they really appear. You accomplish that by manipulating or enlarging the image on the paper.' He drew a simple trend chart on the top of a new flipchart sheet:

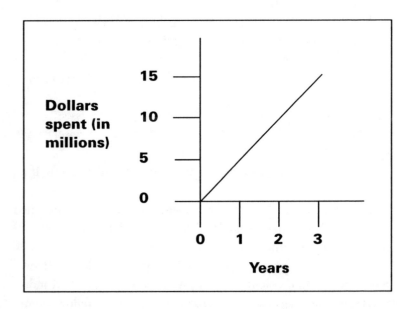

'Now I shall reduce the steepness of the curve by increasing the distance between the years.'

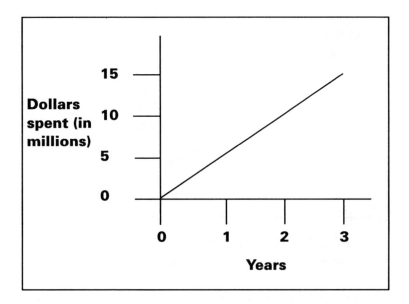

'Perhaps you want to increase the steepness of the curve. You can consolidate the years to increase the steepness of the chart, thereby making the situation appear worse. Notice that $15 million is spent over a three-year timeframe in each chart. Nothing's really changed.'

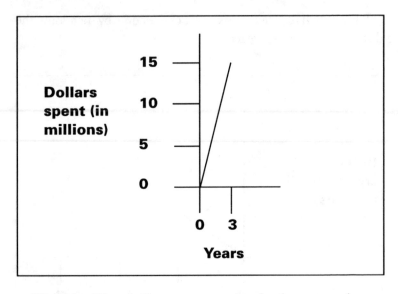

'Wow', said David. 'I see your point. Just by the way you lay out your illustration you can give an incorrect impression. Never thought about that.'

'Well, that's it for illustrations.' Demosthenes tore the pages from the flipchart and handed them to David.

'Demost, I must tell you that I learned a lot of good stuff today.' David then took a deep sigh. 'But I need some more instructions on another subject.'

'I know', said Demosthenes. 'Answering questions.'

'That's right', said David. 'Can we discuss that now?'

'Listen. You work on answering questions and I'll work on asking them. And I've got one for you.'

'Oh', said David. 'I see.'

'Do you and your mother want to come here for dinner tonight to learn about answering questions?'

'What do you think?' said David, chuckling over the fact that he answered a question with a question.

# Chapter 27

'Wow!' said David as he walked through the front door of the lounge.

'Oh my', said his mother, Liz.

'Welcome, my friends', said Demosthenes, rising from a table complete with all the accoutrements of fine dining. A salmon-coloured silk tablecloth. Two large silver candle holders with burning candles. Place settings for three, each a complete set of expensive linens, bone china, crystal glassware and sterling silverware. Bowls of fruit, olives, cheeses, bread, *tzatziki*[1] and a bottle of *retsina*[2] occupied the centre of the table. Above the table was a huge chandelier that appeared like hanging diamonds sparkling in the light of the lounge. In a far corner of the lounge was an old man singing and playing on a *bouzouki*.[3] Standing by the table in a white outfit with a towel draped over his arm was Demetri.

---

[1]*Tzatziki*: cucumber and yogurt dip.
[2]*Retsina*: a Greek wine having a resinous, tangy flavour.
[3]*Bouzouki*: an instrument similar to a banjo used for playing folk music.

David watched as Demost reached for Liz's right hand, took a bow and kissed it.

'It is so good that you attended our dinner', said Demosthenes.

'Oh my', Liz said in a weak voice.

David then shook hands with the Greek. 'Not bad, Demost. Not bad at all.'

Demosthenes led them to the table. He helped Liz to be seated at one end of the table. He then seated himself at the other end.

David sat at the side of the table. 'When's dinner?'

'David', snapped his mother. 'Mind your manners. It will be here soon enough.'

Demosthenes lightly clapped his hands and Demetri came to him. 'Champagne, everyone?'

David and Liz nodded.

'Very good', said Demosthenes. 'Would you please, Demetri?'

Demetri pulled a bottle from an ice bucket standing next to the table. He removed the cork and poured the champagne as they talked.

'So, David', said the Greek orator. 'Have you thought about what we discussed during our last meeting?'

'You mean about illustrations?' David asked. 'Sure. I just have to start work on the next presentation.'

'David told me all about it', said Liz. 'He sure has learned a lot from you.'

'Why thank you, Liz.' Demosthenes smiled. 'It is a pleasure to have you here this evening, Liz. It adds so much to the ... the ... atmosphere.'

'Oh my', said Liz, lightly patting her hands at the base of her neck and blushing. 'You're very flattering.'

'No, I mean it.' Demosthenes picked up his champagne glass and raised it. 'To my very good friends, Liz and David. As we say in Greece, *Yiassas!*'

David and Liz did the same.

'And I would like to propose a toast', said Liz, 'to a gentleman, great orator, and a wonderful person.'

Demosthenes sat silent and still.

David raised his glass and then Demosthenes followed. 'I never thought I'd see Demosthenes at a loss for words.' David started to laugh.

Liz and Demosthenes laughed, too.

'So tonight', said Demosthenes, 'let's discuss how to handle questions and answers.' He rose from the table and walked to the stage. He slid the flipchart stand from behind the curtain. 'Questions and answers', he said as he wrote. 'This is about the hardest part of giving effective presentations. That's because it's more art than science. Since you're giving an explanatory presentation, I'm sure you'll be asked questions that you'd better know how to handle. The best way to do that is to prepare yourself for the questions and practise responding to them. Otherwise, *poulaki mou*, you'll give the wrong impression.'

'That's right', said Liz, pointing her finger at David. 'You don't get a second chance to make a first impression.'

'Yeah, I know', said David. 'I don't want to give the impression that I don't know what I'm talking about and destroy my *ethos*.'

'And your *pathos*', said Demosthenes. 'So with that understanding in mind, what are some of the benefits of having questions and answers during or after a presentation?'

'Let's see ... ' David took a sip of his champagne. 'I'd say one benefit is to clarify a point for someone.'

'Good', said Demosthenes as he wrote. 'Another?'

'I have one', said Liz. 'I mean, if I can say something.'

'Mom, this is between Demost and me', said David.

'It's okay', said Demosthenes, looking at David. 'Your mother is a very intelligent woman. I'm sure a lady of her calibre can handle this conversation.' He turned his gaze towards Liz and winked. 'Please, I'd love to hear what you have to say.'

'Oh my', said Liz. 'I was just going to say that it helps you to build and sustain a communicative relationship with the audience.'

'A very excellent point', said Demosthenes, writing.

'Yeah', said David, crossing his arms. 'I was going to say the same thing.'

'Now, are there any other benefits?' asked Demosthenes.

Liz raised her hand.

'Liz, you can speak any time. You don't have to raise your hand', said Demosthenes. 'You have a very pleasant voice to listen to.'

David looked up towards the ceiling as he tightened his arms.

'Demost', said Liz, 'I'd say that it gives the presenter an opportunity to impart additional ideas and information to the audience.'

'Excellent, Liz. Just simply excellent. I'm so glad you were able to attend.' Demosthenes looked at David. 'Aren't you?'

David nodded.

'Oh dear', said Liz. 'I am, too.' She smiled at the Greek and then at David.

'Yeah, I'm really glad.' David uncrossed his arms as his eyes met his mother's. He then looked at Demosthenes. 'I think there's another benefit. It's somewhat related to the last point.'

'Yes, David', said Demosthenes, waiting to scribble. 'And that is?'

'It gives you the opportunity to repeat and reinforce important comments or concepts introduced during the presentation.'

Demosthenes wrote and said: 'Good point.'

'That's my son', said Liz, winking at David.

'Now it's time to discuss the nuts and bolts of answering questions effectively. Are you ready?'

A short silence ensued. Then Demosthenes spoke. 'That's precisely my first point. After a question is asked, you need to pause before responding. The idea behind that is what?'

'It shows that you're giving serious consideration to the question', said Liz.

'Excellent', said Demosthenes, writing. 'Anything else?'

'Yeah', said David. 'It gives you time to formulate a response that truly answers the question in a way that satisfies the person.'

'Good. Very good', said Demosthenes. 'Another point is to tell the audience when they can ask questions.'

'Good point', said David. 'I failed to do that before the New Projects Council. It caused some frustration initially. I'll be sure to remember this point.'

'Great', said Demosthenes. 'You might also announce some ground rules for questioning.'

'Like what?' Liz asked.

'Well', said Demosthenes, 'you might say that you'd appreciate short questions. Or you might ask the audience to write down the questions and hand them to you. Another rule might be restricting the time for a question and answer session.'

Demosthenes continued to write as he spoke. 'Now let's discuss a little more how you can handle a question. We've already talked about pausing before responding. What else can you do?'

David looked at his mother and shrugged his shoulders. He noticed her nodding her head.

'My son may not have any more ideas but I do', said Liz, looking at David and then at Demosthenes. 'You can rephrase a question.'

'What does that achieve?' asked David, feeling defensive against his own mother.

'Good one, Liz.' Demosthenes wrote on the flipchart. 'That will help you better understand the question and, I might add, give you time to develop an adequate answer.'

David shifted in his chair. 'I'd like to add that you don't necessarily have to rephrase but request that the questioner rephrase his question for further clarification.'

'Good stuff, as you say', said Demosthenes. 'You both have the right idea. But you've forgotten another way to handle questions. Any idea?'

'I'm sorry', said David. 'This champagne has my mind wandering. Could you repeat the question?'

'Don't need to', said Demosthenes. 'You did it for me. You repeated the question!'

'That's very witty, Demost', said Liz, chuckling. 'Isn't it, David?'

'Yeah', said David. 'Really witty. I repeated the question for him.'

'Asking the questioner to repeat the question makes good sense', said Demosthenes. 'You understand the question better, gain enough time to formulate a reasonable response, and make sure the message hasn't been too altered by the filters when you heard the questioner's phrasing of the question. Another way is for you to repeat the question. That's in case some people couldn't hear it.'

David took a gulp from his champagne glass. 'What if … what if … you don't know the answer?'

'I don't know the answer to that question', said Demosthenes.

'I beg your pardon?' Liz asked.

'You don't know?' asked David, dropping his jaw.

Demosthenes smiled. 'Oh, I can be cruel. Are you with me? I don't know the answer. In other words, it's okay to admit that you don't know the answer.'

'But it'll make me look silly', said David.

'But it'll make you look worse pretending you know the answer', said Demost, pointing his finger upward, 'because you may give an incorrect answer or look as if you're faking it. Then your *ethos* disappears.'

'Demost is right, you know', said Liz, reaching across and squeezing her son's hand. 'It's better to be honest.'

'There are some ways to handle questions that you can't handle', said Demosthenes.

'There are?' David asked.

'Listen to Demost', said Liz, pointing at her son.

David nodded. 'Yes, mom.'

Demosthenes continued to speak as he wrote. 'One popular way is to ask if anyone in the audience knows the answer. What's the benefit of that?'

'You build a closer bridge with the audience', said David.

'That's right', said Demosthenes. 'What else?'

'It takes some of the burden off you to appear as the expert', said David.

'That's my son', said Liz. 'He's such a good boy.'

'There's another approach to handling questions you can't answer', said the Greek. 'And that's to write down the question and promise to send the person the answer. There's just one catch to that approach.'

'I know', said Liz. 'You'd better make sure that you follow up with the answer in the near future.'

'That's right. It's the courteous thing to do and adds to your credibility', said Demosthenes. 'Now for one last point about handling questions. Always give short, direct answers. Never give convoluted and wordy responses. Otherwise, you'll lose the questioner and probably the entire audience.' Demosthenes scribbled a few words on the flipchart. He reached into his frock pocket, removed some pebbles and tossed them into his mouth. He then spat them all into a spittoon, making a repetitive sound like a machine gun.

'Wow!' said David, applauding. 'That was some of the best rapid firing I've seen you do yet.'

'Oh my', said Liz. 'That was fascinating.'

Demosthenes took a bow. 'I did that for one reason and one reason only.'

'And that is?' asked David.

'To let Demetri know that it's time to serve dinner', said Demosthenes, tearing off the pages from the flipchart, rolling them up and handing them to David. 'It's time to feast on lamb and drink *retsina*.'

# Chapter 28

'What a feast', said David to his mother as they opened the door to their apartment. 'The lamb was great.'

'The whole evening was great', said Liz with a sigh.

David looked at his mother as he stepped aside to let her in first. 'You wouldn't happen to be falling for him, would you?'

'Me?' asked Liz as she stepped inside. 'He's cute. That's all, David. No one can replace your father.'

'Sure mom. Sure.' David closed the door behind him. 'Well, I guess I better start work on my presentation.'

'But it's late. It's past your bedtime.'

'Not much time left', said David as he closed the door behind him and headed towards the study. 'All I have is tomorrow night to practise.'

'Well, good night.'

'Good night, mom.' David entered the study and closed the door behind him. He taped the flipchart sheets on the wall along with the many others. He sat at his desk studying them for a few minutes. He took some paper and a pencil and developed a rough agenda for the next presentation.

# AGENDA

- *Introduction*
  - *Purpose*
  - *Scope*

- *Background*

- *Goals*
  - *Hospital facility*
  - *Hospital ship*

- *Requirements*

- *Conclusion*

- *Next steps*

After drafting the introduction and the background, he developed a sketch of the floor plans for the hospital and the hospital ship.

Not bad, he thought. Not bad at all. He looked at the flipchart sheet containing the main points about illustrations.

'Bother', he said to himself. 'I need a title for both the ship and hospital complex diagrams. Let's see ... they have a logical flow ... use plenty of white space ... as simple as I can make them ... appears to follow the seven plus two rule ... gives an actual portrayal of what to build ... I don't know about the print size yet ... '

He finished the remaining sections of the presentation. He looked at the clock. It's late, he thought. One-thirty. I'll get up early and put all this stuff in the computer. Then I'll call Demosthenes and see if I can have a practice session tomorrow night. David turned out the light in the room and went to bed feeling more confident than ever.

# Chapter 29

David had worked the entire morning on the presentation, skipping breakfast. He had just about finished when the phone rang.

'Hello. Michaels here.'

'It's me', said an all too familiar voice.

'Demost!' said David, excitedly. 'I've just finished my pitch. It's all done.'

'It is?'

'Yeah. And it looks pretty good if I say so myself', said David as he watched each page ease out from the printer.

'I won't burst your bubble', said the Greek. 'But it's not over until it's over. You still have to practise and perform.'

'Yeah', said David with a sigh. 'I know.' He took a deep breath. 'Why did you call?'

'I have an idea. I want you to go to a local university with me and attend some classes.'

'Do what?' asked David. 'I can't. I have to practise.'

'You have plenty of time for that. Besides, you'll get some great tips attending these classes. You'll experience the agony and ecstasy of explanatory presentations. And I know of no better place for that experience than a university.'

'But I've been to college', said David.

'How long ago?'

'Ten years or so.'

'See you at the entrance of Richards Hall in one hour.'

'But Demost', said David. 'I don't have … '

A loud click echoed in his ear.

David saw Demosthenes standing at the entrance of a huge brick building. Students passed him and streamed inside. 'Demost, don't you think this is a bit too much? I mean … '

'Follow me', said Demosthenes, dragging David's arm. Within seconds, David found himself inside a large auditorium filled with students.

'We'll be able to sit here in the back row and nobody will notice us. We can whisper to each other as the professor speaks. One of the nice things about being in an audience of three hundred is that you become anonymous.'

David noticed a thin, frail man standing behind a podium. Next to the podium was an overhead projector. 'What class is this?'

'The sign outside the door said it was first-year Quantum Mechanics.'

'Well', said David, 'this will either be the best class I ever attended or the worst. I imagine you picked him for a reason.'

'I do everything for a reason', said Demosthenes, smiling. 'You should know that by now.'

The professor spoke. He rambled for five minutes about the new addition to his home. Then he moved into the subject of quantum mechanics.

David listened for about ten minutes. 'I haven't a clue what he's saying', he whispered. 'He's using a bunch of words I've never heard of. And they're not even physics terms.'

Demosthenes nodded. 'What else have you observed?'

'He's talking with the overhead projector running but hasn't used a slide.'

The professor then walked back and forth in front of the podium with his hands deep in his pockets.

David watched as the hundreds of heads in front of him moved non-stop and in tandem from left to right and right to left.

'The professor moves too fast; he reminds me of Hermes, the god of motion. If he keeps moving that way', said Demosthenes, 'I bet their heads will fall off.'

David chuckled. 'Yeah, and if he pushes his hands any deeper into his pockets his pants will fall down, too.'

The professor stopped in front of the overhead projector. He turned his back to the audience and took a slide from the podium. He placed it on the projector; the image showed on the screen at an angle. The professor paced back and forth.

'What a walkie-talkie', observed Demosthenes. 'Now watch him explain that highly sophisticated drawing that looks like it was created by a five-year-old.'

David squinted to read the print. Even the lines on the drawing were hard to see.

The students began scribbling the image in their notebooks. The professor concluded the review of the diagram without even pointing to it.

'Learning anything?' Demosthenes asked.

'Sure am', said David. 'I'm learning how *not* to give an explanatory presentation.'

'Excellent. Now keep observing.'

One of the students raised a hand. The professor continued to look at the floor, pacing back and forth with his hands in his pockets. Other hands went up but the professor never looked up. Soon, the hands fell.

David looked round the audience. Many students read books. Others passed notes. Still others looked at each other and smirked.

The professor stopped pacing. He looked up and asked why there hadn't been any questions so far. He admonished the students for not expressing an interest in the subject.

'Boy', said David. 'This guy's got style.'

Demosthenes pointed to a young man raising his hand. 'Watch this.'

The professor interrupted the student several times as the young man tried to ask the question. The old man laughed as he rephrased the question for the student. The rest of the students also laughed.

'I don't think they're laughing at the question', observed David.

'I think you're right', said Demosthenes. 'They're laughing at the young man.'

The professor asked if there were any other questions. Not one hand rose. The professor noted aloud that he must be getting his point across. He continued to talk.

About a minute passed before the professor showed another slide of a diagram.

'What do you notice about this work of art?' asked Demosthenes.

'There's no title for one thing', said David. 'It doesn't seem to have any logical flow to it. It has more than nine items in it. There's not much white space. And the print is hard to see because the ink is light and the letters and numbers are small. And the professor doesn't even refer to it as he speaks.'

The bell finally rang. The professor rambled at a faster pace in an obvious effort to cover his remaining material. The students rose from their seats as the professor spoke.

'Come on', said Demosthenes. 'Let's go.'

David followed the Greek into another auditorium filled with about two hundred students.

'Hope you like macroeconomics', said Demosthenes.

'About as much as I like quantum mechanics', said David.

The professor, a tall man with curly red hair, opened the session with an agenda flashed on a screen from the overhead projector. He discussed the main points for the hour, the supply and demand curve. He turned off the overhead projector, noted the purpose of the class and what students should expect. He also said that questions were welcome any time.

'What do you think?' whispered Demosthenes.

'No comparison so far with the quantum mechanics', said David.

The professor stood behind the podium. From time to time, he moved away from it to emphasize a point. His mannerisms came naturally and accentuated what he had to say.

David watched as the professor turned on the overhead projector and stood so that he faced the audience and did not block the image on the screen. The professor removed a pointer from his shirt pocket and extended it. He discussed the contents of the supply and demand curve as he moved the pointer across the image.

'No doubt about it', said David. 'This guy knows how to communicate complex topics. He doesn't use jargon. Doesn't talk down to the audience. Uses the overhead projector really well. Expresses himself clearly. Tells the audience when to ask questions.'

'This is the real thing', said Demosthenes.

David nodded as he directed his attention to the professor.

A student raised his hand and asked a lengthy question. The professor paused for a second and repeated the question more succinctly.

'Now that's how to handle a question', said Demosthenes.

Other students joined in and asked their questions. Sometimes the professor repeated or rephrased the question while at other times the students did it themselves. In some cases, students volunteered to answer another student's question.

The professor glanced at his watch as he continued to present his subject within the last remaining minutes. He finally presented the homework assignments and addressed remaining questions from the audience.

The bell rang.

'Wow', said David, 'I sure hope I can give a presentation like that.'

'You can', said Demosthenes. 'But with practice. It doesn't come overnight.' He rose from the seat and headed for the exit.

David followed. 'How much do you practise?'

'Until I can do it right.'

'But how do you know when you've practised enough? You could be practising forever.'

'Just like Sisyphus.'

'Like who?' asked David.

'Sisyphus. Zeus condemned Sisyphus to push a large boulder up a hill. Just when he reached the apex, the boulder would fall down the slope. Sisyphus would have to start again pushing the rock up the hillside.'

'What a dismal fate', said David in a morose voice.

'Fortunately, you can avoid such a fate. Let me tell you how I practise. As I told you earlier, sometimes I used to hide in a cave for days before giving a speech, shaved only half my face so I'd be forced to stay until I'd practised my speech to the point when I felt I was ready to give it.'

'Oh yeah', said David, 'I guess I'd better start practising as soon as I can. I give my presentation tomorrow at nine a.m.' They left the entrance from Richards Hall and walked within a stream of college students. 'Mind if I practise with you?'

Demosthenes coughed. 'I'd like to. But I have a very special engagement tonight.'

'Huh? Demosthenes, I need you.' David felt a wave of insecurity overcome him. He grabbed the Greek by the arm and

153

looked him square in the eye. 'I need you to give me the necessary feedback on my dry runs.'

Demosthenes shook his head and backed away. 'Sorry. Tonight's a special night. You'll do fine on your own. Besides, I always practised by myself. It turned out better. I was less self-conscious.'

'But you told me earlier that it is best to practise in front of other people.'

Demosthenes agreed and then abruptly said, 'Sorry. Today's visit to the university should help you a lot.'

'But tomorrow morning? What about tomorrow morning?' asked David. 'Will you be there?'

'Who knows, David? Who knows?' Demosthenes then said, 'I suggest the sooner you get home the more time you'll have to practise. Good day, *poulaki mou.*'

David froze with fear as he watched the Greek orator disappear into the crowd of students. For the first time in his life he found himself in a crowd yet still felt alone.

And abandoned.

# Chapter 30

Before David could insert his key the door swung open. In front of him stood a woman that he had to look at twice to recognize. 'Where are you going?'

'I have a very important engagement tonight', said Liz.

'You too?' asked David, still standing in the doorway of his apartment. 'Yeah, it must be quite an engagement. I haven't seen you dressed like that in ten years. It must be some engagement.'

'It is, son. So please excuse me.'

'You're coming back early I hope', said David, standing to the side of the entrance.

'Back by eleven-thirty', she said, passing. 'There's some lasagne in the refrigerator.'

'But that late?' he asked, watching her pass. 'I can't wait that long. I need you for my rehearsals.'

'I can't help you tonight, son. This engagement means a lot to me', she said as she descended the stairway. 'You'll just have to be on your own. I'm sure you'll do fine.'

'Yeah sure', he said. 'Just fine.' He closed the door behind him.

David settled down and ate his dinner. It was now eight o'clock and he decided to start practising.

He stood before a full-length mirror to practise his body movements. He tried to be conscious of any distracting mannerisms and to coordinate gestures with his words. He also focused on his stature, ensuring that he stood with his shoulders back and his head held high. Not bad, he thought. Not bad at all. After going through the presentation in front of the mirror three times, he decided he should now work on his voice.

David went to the study and pulled a portable audio tape recorder from his desk. He spoke into the device three times until he felt comfortable that he sounded natural, not contrived, but also avoided 'ahs' and 'you knows'. He made sure too that he sounded confident, speaking with a clear, strong voice.

Although he felt he was making progress, he still lacked a sense of completeness; of synchronicity. He thought hard. He had practised refining his poise and body language before the mirror and worked on his vocal delivery using a tape recorder. Yet, he still felt he lacked any sense of unity.

Then he remembered his newest purchase – a camcorder and tripod in his bedroom. He rushed into the room, fetched the equipment and set it up in his kitchen. He put a small box on the table to serve as a podium and a still smaller box nearby to serve as a mock overhead projector. He turned the machine on and practised several times before the camera, pretending that it was a member of the audience.

After his third rehearsal, he inserted the video cassette in a player in the living room and watched his performances, keeping in mind all the Pebbles of Wisdom Demost had imparted to him.

David gave a deep sigh of relief as he noticed with each successive practice, just as the Greek orator had said, he improved. Practice really does make perfect, thought David.

He turned off the video cassette recorder and started nodding off in his chair. The sound of a turning door knob woke him.

'Mom', he said, looking at his watch. 'It's twelve-thirty.'

'You weren't staying up for me?' she asked as she closed the door behind her and entered the living room.

'No', he said. 'I've been practising. That's all.'

'Well, if you're giving your presentation at nine o'clock tomorrow then you had better go to bed.'

'I'd like to give one rehearsal in front of you so you can ask me a few questions and I can practise responding to them.'

'Okay', she said. 'But that's it. Where?'

'In the kitchen.'

They went into the kitchen. After giving his presentation, he practised answering a few questions. 'Well, how did I do?'

'Great, son. You did just great. You're getting as good as your father.'

'I am?' asked David, his voice rising.

She nodded. 'Now let's go to bed. You've got a big day tomorrow. And I'm tired from going out.'

'Going out?' David asked.

Liz remained silent.

'With whom?' he persisted.

'It's late, son.' She rose from her chair. 'Good luck tomorrow morning. We know you'll do fine.'

'We?' asked David. 'Who's we?'

'Goodnight, son.' She went into her bedroom and closed the door.

'We?' he asked himself as he went to his bedroom. 'We?'

# Chapter 31

The same mahogany doors as at the last presentation swung open. He followed the same shapely secretary as she led the way to the same dais. Only this time, the audience was different – larger. There were seven people.

David exchanged introductions and proceeded to the podium with handouts under his left arm. Boy, he thought, it's so warm in here. And where is Demosthenes?

He laid the handouts on the inside shelf of the podium. He checked to ensure that the bulb in the projector worked and that the first slide was focused. He turned off the projector and got ready to speak when a gentle knock was heard.

A member of the audience asked David to open the door. David did so, holding the large brass handle. As the door eased open, David screwed up his eyes for a clearer look. 'What the ... ?'

'I'm here to fix the ventilation problem in this conference room.' The face and voice were all too familiar.

'De ... '

'Where's the thermostat?' asked Demosthenes, pushing his way past David with his tool belt jingling.

A member of the Steering Committee pointed to the device in the opposite corner of the room. Demosthenes hurried to it.

'We can't hold up the presentation for this', said one listener.

'Agreed', said another. 'If we delay too much we'll fall behind schedule. Proceed, Mr Michaels.'

David approached the podium. He looked at the people behind the dais and his blood rushed. His palms became moist. His heart pounded.

'My name is David Michaels. Like yourselves, I have experience with working inside the Yuggenheim Corporation and its Foundation. It is, therefore, with great pleasure that I shall be explaining to everyone here what I propose to do for the Love is for Everyone project – or LIFE for short.'

David turned on the overhead projector and showed the agenda.

---

### YUGGENHEIM FOUNDATION

### LOVE IS FOR EVERYONE PROPOSAL

---

**Love is for Everyone Proposal**


**David Michaels**


**October 29, 19XX**

---

# YUGGENHEIM FOUNDATION

## LOVE IS FOR EVERYONE PROPOSAL

### AGENDA

☞ **Introduction**

☞ **Background**

☞ **Goals**

☞ **Requirements**

☞ **Conclusion**

☞ **Next Steps**

160

He gave a quick overview of the agenda and said: 'Feel free to ask questions any time during the presentation.' He caught a glimpse of Demosthenes in a far corner of the room.

He showed the next slide.

---

### YUGGENHEIM FOUNDATION

### LOVE IS FOR EVERYONE PROPOSAL

---

### INTRODUCTION

### PURPOSE

Set up hospital facility site and hospital ship to traverse the Amazon Basin

---

'The purpose of the project', he continued as he stepped to the side of the podium, being careful not to block the image, 'is to establish a hospital facility and provide a hospital ship in the dense jungles of the Amazon in South America.'

He replaced the slide with a new one.

'The scope is narrow', he said, making sure not to lean on the podium and maintaining eye contact with the audience. 'It's to provide high-quality healthcare services to the at-risk and underprivileged children living in the dense foliage of the Amazon Basin.'

He replaced the slide with another.

```
┌─────────────────────────────────────────────┐
│                                               │
│          YUGGENHEIM FOUNDATION                │
│                                               │
│                                               │
│       LOVE IS FOR EVERYONE PROPOSAL           │
│                                               │
├─────────────────────────────────────────────┤
├─────────────────────────────────────────────┤
│                                               │
│                BACKGROUND                     │
│                                               │
│                                               │
│       Approved by New Projects Council        │
│                                               │
│                                               │
│                                               │
│                                               │
│                                               │
│                                               │
└─────────────────────────────────────────────┘
```

'But before I explain what I propose to do', said David, returning to the podium, 'I'd like to share some background information with you.

'As you know, this project received the initial approval of the New Projects Council. This is significant because it represents the beginning of a long journey from inception to implementation.'

The next slide went up.

## YUGGENHEIM FOUNDATION

## LOVE IS FOR EVERYONE PROPOSAL

### GOALS

Build and deploy
hospital facility site

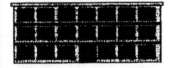

☞ Develop and request
bid proposals to
build the hospital

☞ Employ modern
equipment and
technology

☞ Hire professional
healthcare staff

☞ Ensure sufficient
medical supplies

☞ Provide adequate
space for patients

'For your information', said David, watching Demost's beaming face, 'there are several goals to accomplish in regard to the hospital facility.'

David withdrew the pointer from his shirt pocket and pointed to the first item. 'First, invite quotes to build the hospital.' He then moved to the next item. 'And obtain the best equipment possible.'

A member of the audience asked a lengthy question.

David paused briefly. 'For the benefit of understanding your question allow me to paraphrase what you asked. You essentially asked what types of skill will be required to construct the hospital. Is that correct?'

The listener nodded. David looked at Demosthenes and the Greek smiled back. 'I believe that the workforce will consist of local construction workers who are familiar with the construction practices and architecture of the region. These will not necessarily be highly skilled workers but those who can do the work. Of course, I'll need the services of an architect.'

David finished presenting the goals of the facility and then discussed the goals of the ship while showing the next slide.

## YUGGENHEIM FOUNDATION

## LOVE IS FOR EVERYONE PROPOSAL

### GOALS

Acquire and deploy
hospital ship

☞ Develop and request
bid proposals to
acquire the hospital
ship

☞ Employ modern
equipment and
technology

☞ Hire professional
healthcare staff

☞ Hire professional ship
crew

☞ Ensure sufficient
medical supplies

☞ Provide adequate
space for patients,
staff and crew

166

After explaining the goals of the ship, David placed the next slide on the platen of the overhead projector.

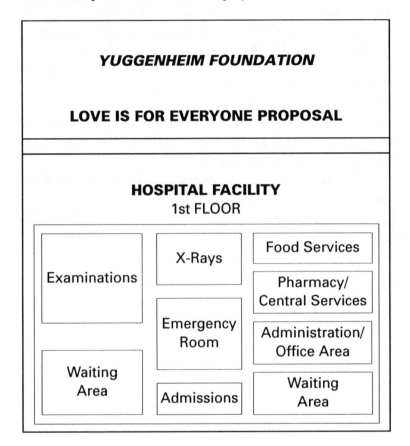

*YUGGENHEIM FOUNDATION*

**LOVE IS FOR EVERYONE PROPOSAL**

**HOSPITAL FACILITY**
1st FLOOR

| | | |
|---|---|---|
| Examinations | X-Rays | Food Services |
| | | Pharmacy/ Central Services |
| | Emergency Room | Administration/ Office Area |
| Waiting Area | | Waiting Area |
| | Admissions | |

'Keeping the goals in mind for both the hospital and the ship, I'll now explain what the facility will look like.' David positioned himself next to the screen so that he faced the audience and pointed to the upper left section of the diagram. He looked at Demosthenes who gave a thumbs-up to express his approval. 'The facility will have three floors. The first one, as you can see here', he continued as he pointed but maintained eye contact with the audience, 'has an examination room, a waiting area, X-ray room, emergency room, admissions section, food services, a pharmacy, administrative office area and another waiting area.'

David asked whether the audience had any other questions.

One person spoke. 'Why are there two waiting areas?'

David paused. Then he replied while pointing to the diagram and then focusing on the questioner: 'One is to accommodate those who must see the doctor while the other is for handling administrative matters. By having two you allow for greater utilization of floor space.' He looked at the rest of the audience. 'Are there any other questions?'

He waited several seconds before continuing and replacing the slide with another.

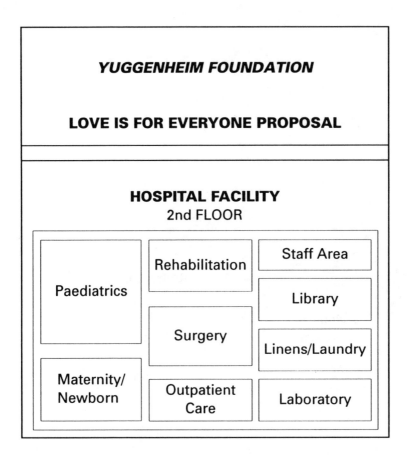

'This diagram shows the layout for the second floor', he continued, making sure that the slide was straight on the platen and remained in focus. 'It will have rooms for paediatrics, rehabilitation, surgery, maternity and newborn, and outpatient care. It will also have a staff area for breaks, a library, laundry and a laboratory.' David continued to face the audience, only looking periodically at the image on the screen to ensure that he was pointing at the right room in the diagram.

'Any questions?' He waited briefly before showing the next slide.

169

```
┌─────────────────────────────────────────────────┐
│                                                  │
│          YUGGENHEIM FOUNDATION                   │
│                                                  │
│        LOVE IS FOR EVERYONE PROPOSAL             │
│                                                  │
├─────────────────────────────────────────────────┤
│                                                  │
│              HOSPITAL FACILITY                   │
│                 3rd FLOOR                         │
│   ┌──────────┐  ┌───────────────────────────┐   │
│   │          │  │                           │   │
│   │          │  │      Intensive Care       │   │
│   │          │  │                           │   │
│   │ Special  │  └───────────────────────────┘   │
│   │ Services │  ┌───────────────────────────┐   │
│   │          │  │                           │   │
│   │          │  │     Intermediate Care     │   │
│   │          │  │                           │   │
│   └──────────┘  └───────────────────────────┘   │
└─────────────────────────────────────────────────┘
```

'The third floor, as you can see, contains three large rooms.' He continued to face the audience while pointing at the first room. 'The first one is for special services.' David spotted a hand jerking up in the audience. 'Yes sir?'

'When you say special services what do you mean?' said the man in a soft voice.

David looked over at Demosthenes for a sign. He noticed the old Greek bringing his hand to his ear. 'Did everyone hear his question?' asked David.

Everyone nodded.

'Good question', continued David. He paused for a few seconds and then spoke. 'By special services I mean treatments related to contagious diseases, psychiatric problems and the quarantine of advanced medical cases.'

He looked over at the Greek faking a yawn.

David pointed to the slide image and spoke as he turned his attention to the audience. He noticed that some weren't even listening; they were thumbing through papers or doodling. 'The second room is for intensive care, that is, to handle critical health situations. The last room is for intermediate care, such as for patients who require care and observation. Are there any questions?'

He paused for several seconds as he looked at Demosthenes.

The Greek placed his hand behind his right ear again and then yawned.

'I'd like now to discuss the docking area for the hospital ship.' He showed the next slide.

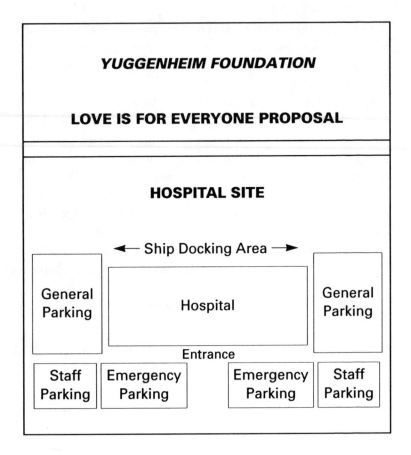

'As you can see here', said David, removing the pointer from his shirt pocket, extracting it and using it to point at the image, 'the hospital facility will be located close to the docking area. This will enable easier unloading of patients and easier loading of supplies. There will also be general and emergency parking areas for people who can afford cars and emergency vehicles. The ship docking area shown at the top is, of course, on the Amazon River.'

David noticed that the Greek faked another yawn. He asked if anyone had any questions. As there were none, he displayed the next slide.

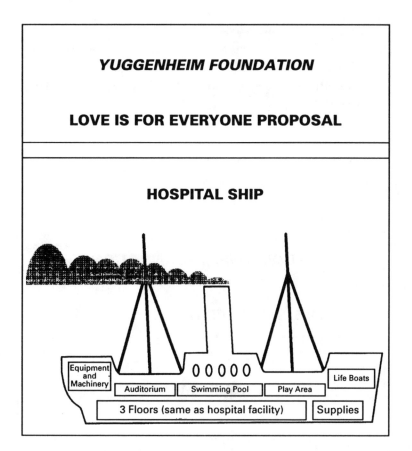

'Next, I'd like to describe what the hospital ship will contain.' David pointed at the upper deck and worked his way down. Finished, he asked if there were any questions.

A long pause ensued until one listener spoke. 'What is the length of the vessel?'

David took a deep breath and said, 'Approximately 180 metres long and 60 metres wide. Not exactly the *Titanic* but big enough not to sink.'

The audience chuckled.

David put the pointer back into his pocket. 'Are there any more questions about the ship?'

'Proceed', said a man, looking at his watch.

'Yes, continue', added another. 'The next presentation is scheduled to begin shortly. By the way', added the man, looking at Demosthenes, 'have you finished working on the ventilation system? It's cooler in here now.'

'Just finishing a few details', replied Demosthenes. 'Just a few more minutes.'

'Continue', said the man to David.

David displayed the next slide.

---

## YUGGENHEIM FOUNDATION

## LOVE IS FOR EVERYONE PROPOSAL

---

## REQUIREMENTS

☞ People

☞ Materials/Supplies

☞ Equipment

☞ Facilities

☞ Budget

---

'Now the construction of the facility and the ship will not appear at a snap of a finger. It will require people, materials, equipment, temporary facilities and, of course, money.'

'Have you done any calculations on the costs involved?' asked a listener.

David paused. He knew that his response could possibly affect the vote of the Executive Steering Committee.

'Ah ... Let's see ... ' David groped for an answer but none came. He looked over to where Demosthenes stood.

The Greek moved his lips but no words came out.

'I ... I ... '

'I see', said the man who had asked the money question.

'I believe the question of money is not an issue for this committee to consider. At least not officially', said another listener. 'The Board of Directors has responsibility for that.' The man looked at David and asked, 'Nevertheless, my colleague here raises an interesting point. Have you made any preliminary cost estimates and, if so, what are they?'

David felt a lump come to his throat. How could I be so naïve as not to calculate any costs? he thought. Should I admit that I don't know? Then he remembered what Demosthenes had said about admitting not knowing the answer. 'No, not at this time', he said. 'But I will give you an answer by close of business today.' He looked at Demosthenes and noticed the Greek orator nodding in approval. 'Are there any further questions regarding requirements?'

After several agonizing seconds, David showed the next slide.

```
YUGGENHEIM FOUNDATION


LOVE IS FOR EVERYONE PROPOSAL
```

```
CONCLUSION


☞   Basic healthcare services

☞   Broad scope of requirements
```

He returned to the podium but did not clutch it or lean on it. 'Essentially, the LIFE project seeks to provide basic healthcare services to the unfortunate in Brazil. But to accomplish that will mean fulfilling a broad scope of requirements. Building a hospital facility and ship will not be an easy task.' He took a deep breath and changed to the next slide.

```
┌─────────────────────────────────────────────┐
│                                             │
│        YUGGENHEIM FOUNDATION                 │
│                                             │
│                                             │
│        LOVE IS FOR EVERYONE PROPOSAL         │
│                                             │
├─────────────────────────────────────────────┤
│                                             │
│                 NEXT STEPS                   │
│                                             │
│                                             │
│      ☞   Approval from Executive            │
│          Steering Committee                  │
│                                             │
│      ☞   Presentation to Board of           │
│          Directors                           │
│                                             │
│                                             │
│                                             │
└─────────────────────────────────────────────┘
```

'There remain three steps to make this project a reality. The first is approval by this committee. The second is to give a presentation before the Board of Directors, resulting in the third step, approval by the Board.'

David turned off the overhead projector and asked for any further questions or comments.

'Mr Michaels', said the man seated at the centre of the dais. 'We shall inform you of our decision tomorrow morning, no later than nine o'clock.'

'I would like to leave you with some hard copies of my presentation', said David as he carried them to the dais and distributed them. He glanced periodically at Demosthenes as he shook hands with his listeners.

As David turned and headed towards the exit, he noticed Demosthenes followed closely behind.

'It was really hot for a while', whispered the Greek with a smirk.

'Yeah', said David, softly. 'But it doesn't seem to be any cooler now.'

# Chapter 32

'Well, what do you think?' asked David.

'About what?' asked Demosthenes, leading the way down a busy pavement.

'About what?' repeated David. 'The presentation. That's what.'

Demosthenes stopped and turned. 'Come with me to the *kafenion* and we'll discuss it.'

'Sounds good to me', David said.

They stepped inside the same coffee shop that they visited after the presentation before the New Projects Council. They ordered their coffee and chatted.

'Okay, Demost', said David, crossing his arms. 'Let me have it.'

'Wrong attitude, *poulaki mou*', said the Greek. 'Wrong attitude.' He reached into his pocket, pulled out some pebbles and popped them in his mouth. 'First, let me start off with what went well. And it did, in general, go well.'

'Really?' asked David, easing his arms down.

Demosthenes nodded. 'Much better than the first presentation. Much, much better.'

'What a relief.'

'In fact, *poulaki mou*, you did so well I have very little to criticize.'

'What went well?' asked David like a child waiting to open a Christmas present.

'For a start, you told the audience when they could ask questions, unlike before. You did not keep the overhead projector running when you didn't have any slides to show. You didn't block images on the screen. You maintained good eye contact. You did not say "ahs" and "you knows" over and over. The slides were easily readable. You didn't lean on the podium or stand still behind it. You paused before answering questions and you rephrased questions well when it was necessary. You handed out copies at the end of the presentation. In short, you did a super job in comparison to the last time.'

'Then I don't need to improve?' asked David.

'I didn't say that', said Demosthenes, spitting a pebble in an ashtray. 'You do have some areas that need improvement.'

'Oh?' David crossed his arms.

'Don't become another Narcissus with me, *poulaki mou*', warned the Greek.

'What did he do?' asked David.

'Let's just say he became so infatuated with himself that he admired his own image reflected in a pool.'

'Okay, Demost. I get the message. Tell me my areas for improvement.'

'Very good. Although you handled most questions well you had trouble with one.'

'Yeah, I really blew that one', said David, knowing which one the Greek meant.

'No, correction. You need to improve. Now you seemed to grope for an answer about the cost. Why is that?'

David bit his lower lip and then spoke. 'I couldn't give him an answer.'

'Fortunately, you salvaged the situation by saying that you didn't know. That made me very proud of you. I'm sure your mother would be too.'

'Yeah, and I owe them an answer', said David.

'Make sure you deliver your promise.'

'You bet. As soon as you've finished I'm going to make the calculations and deliver them.'

'Very good, *poulaki mou*. Very good.' Demosthenes spat a pebble into the ashtray. 'Only one other insight for improvement.'

'What's that?' asked David.

'Your voice. It sometimes was hard to hear. It also sounded monotonous. I noticed that some of the listeners started to yawn and doodle on notebook paper. One person was reading a newspaper. We've got to work on that.'

'Goodness, Demost, was I that boring?'

'Quite honestly, you were no, as you say, dynamo. And you didn't manage to involve the audience very well. Fortunately, you didn't have to give a speech to persuade, even though all presentations require some level of persuasion.'

'That's my next presentation, Demost. If I pass this one', said David. 'I'll go before the Board of Directors for final approval.'

'You know those worry beads I gave you?' asked Demosthenes.

'Yeah. Why?' asked David.

'I'll need them back. Especially if you'll be giving a persuasive presentation.' He then spat the rest of the pebbles in the ashtray.

# Chapter 33

David looked at the clock as he awoke from the ringing of the phone.

'Nine o'clock', he shouted. 'I overslept. Man alive.' He jumped from the bed and reached for the phone.

'Hello?'

'Mr Michaels?' asked a female voice.

'This is he.'

'I'm calling on behalf of the Executive Steering Committee.'

'Yes. Yes.' His blood raced. His palms became moist. His heart pounded.

'The Executive Steering Committee has deferred making a decision.'

'Why?' asked David. His stomach felt as if it was filled with lead.

'They're awaiting information about costs that you had promised them yesterday.'

How could I be so stupid, he thought. How could I forget? He slapped his forehead. 'I'll get them that information immediately … '

'Mr Michaels?'

'Yes?'

'I've just been informed that the Executive Steering Committee reconsidered its decision to defer. They have just made their decision.'

His knees trembled. He fell into the chair next to the phone. He combed his hair with his fingers. 'They did?'

'Yes, sir.'

'And?' he asked in a squeaky voice.

'Well, they were disappointed with the fact that you didn't deliver some cost data you promised.'

Oh no, he thought. It's over. Let me have it, lady. I'm a grown man. I can take it. Just don't prolong the agony. 'Well, I guess it's over.'

'No sir. They granted approval.'

David placed his hand over the receiver and let out a scream. He removed his hand. 'What was the split?'

'Four to three. One gentleman changed his vote from an abstention to pro. You're now scheduled to give your final presentation to the Board of Directors in three days at nine o'clock in conference room A in the same building.'

'Thank you.' David hung up the phone. Just then his bedroom door swung open.

'What's going on?' asked Liz. 'I heard a loud scream.'

'The Executive Steering Committee gave its approval.'

'Is it over now? Did you get the approval you need?'

'No, not yet', said David. 'Now I have to give a presentation before the Board of Directors. If I get their okay, then the project can go ahead.'

'I'm proud of you, son.' She gave him a big hug. 'I think, though, I'd better give Demosthenes a ring. Call it woman's intuition, but the next presentation will be your toughest.'

'Why do *you* have to call him?' David asked.

# Chapter 34

'You're now entering the big league of professional presentations', said Demosthenes. He downed the remaining drops of coffee from his cup. He set the cup back on the table, rose from his chair and climbed on to the Parthenon's stage. He pulled the flipchart stand from behind the curtain. 'Now you're going to play with the big boys and girls.'

'I know', said David, downing the last drops of ouzo in his glass. 'I know.'

'Don't look so glum, *poulaki mou*. You passed the New Projects Council. Then the Executive Steering Committee. Now it's the Board of Directors.'

'This time I have to persuade the Board to approve and authorize expenditures. Everything hinges on that Board's okay. There's no second chance. None.'

'All the more reason, *poulaki mou*, to function in top form. You have to do your best. Getting by will not be enough. Remember, in life usually you first take the test and then get the lesson. You're more fortunate, however. You're having the lessons first. And there won't be a second chance to make a first impression … '

'That's right', said David combing his hair with his fingers. 'The Board requires unanimous approval before it authorizes expenditures. A majority vote is not good enough.'

'Sounds tough to me', said the Greek. 'But you can do it. You can persuade them to your way of thinking. Like Achilles in the Trojan War, you must be brave despite the seemingly insurmountable odds you will face. In the end, Achilles defeated the Trojans, bringing glory to himself and to Greece!' Demosthenes reached into his pocket, removed some pebbles and popped them in his mouth. 'It'll be a mouthful. But you can do it.'

'Sure hope so.' David fell back into his chair. 'This presentation must be persuasive. Really persuasive.'

'Ah, yes', said Demosthenes. 'What's that saying ... Oh yes ... A fool and his money are soon parted.' He chuckled and said, 'And the Board of Directors doesn't want to become a group of fools. So they'll be sceptical all right. A unanimous vote will be tough to win but it happens and there's no reason that it won't.'

'Thanks, Demost.' David poured himself some more ouzo. 'But this is a completely different type of presentation from the others ... '

'Yes and no.'

'Huh?' asked David.

'What I mean is that what you've learned earlier still applies. Nothing really changes. It just involves having a different purpose. A persuasive presentation requires convincing the audience to your way of thinking or opinion and then taking action. You were doing the same to a limited degree in the earlier presentations. The main difference with the current one is that convincing the audience becomes the primary purpose of the presentation, not just informing or explaining something.'

'I see', said David. 'It seems, then, that psychology plays a big role in putting together and giving a persuasive presentation.'

Demosthenes spat a pebble into the spittoon at the base of the flipchart stand. 'Exactly. Everything about the six Pebbles of

Wisdom that I taught you is still applicable. Only psychology plays a more prominent role.' Demosthenes took up a marker and scribbled 'Perspective' at the top of the flipchart. 'Are you ready?'

'Let's see', said David, rubbing his chin. 'Perspective.'

'That's right, *poulaki mou*. Perspective.'

'Right now, I know the Board is looking to spend money', said David. 'The Yuggenheim Corporation had a prosperous year and its Foundation is looking for some good write-offs. They've also expressed an interest in operating in the Amazon.'

Demosthenes scribbled. 'And what about the membership of the Board?'

'Well, the Board consists of very high-ranking executives who focus on the main issues, not the details. They are wizened business men and women who are conservative in nature and outlook and do not make decisions lightly.'

'And what might be their perspective of you, based on what you know about yourself?'

'Me?' asked David, pointing to himself. 'Well, they probably think I'll be no different from just about anybody who also comes to them with a proposal, asking for approval and money. I'll have a slight edge, though, because they know I worked for the Yuggenheim Corporation before and departed with a good, solid track record, especially as a project manager. My youth may pose a problem so I guess they'll look for maturity in my thinking and demeanour. Demosthenes, going through all this for me is really helpful.'

'That's why we're doing it. There's one other consideration when discussing perspective for dealing with persuasive presentations.'

'That', said David, proudly, 'is the physical environment.'

'Correct', said Demosthenes with a smile. 'What are some indicators of an unsatisfactory physical environment?'

'Poor lighting ... room being too warm or cold ... too much background noise ... too many people crammed into a room ... things like that', said David.

'I'd say that's good enough', said Demosthenes, writing. 'Now don't discount the importance of this factor. It can very much impede or improve communications. Some people don't take this seriously enough. But we are all influenced a great deal by our environment. I suggest you take a look at the location where you give your presentation.'

The Greek flipped a page. He drew a diagram. 'You remember this?'

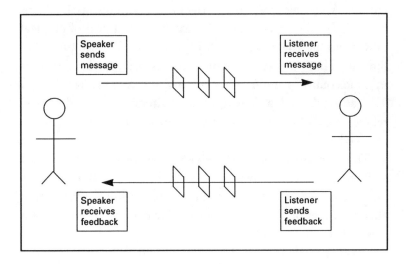

David nodded. 'Yeah. It's the diagram on the communication process.'

'Exactly. In a persuasive presentation, recognizing the role of those filters, such as values and beliefs, becomes very important. They affect the next POW, perception, concerning you and your message.'

'That's right', said David. 'If their perception of me is of a certain kind, for instance, I could be sending subtle or overt messages that activate a filter that helps or hinders the communication process.'

187

'Indeed, it is important to recognize some of the filters that can affect perceptions about you and your message', said Demosthenes as he flipped to a new page and wrote 'Perception' at the top. 'One we have already discussed quite a bit. I'll give you a clue. Playing with a pointer.'

'Distracting mannerisms', David said, snapping his fingers. 'There are plenty of others, like jingling change in your pocket. Moving about like a walkie-talkie.'

'That's right', said the Greek, scribbling away. 'Another one is culture. And sometimes culture ties closely with distracting mannerisms. For instance, some cultures like a great deal of physical movement at the podium while others prefer restrained behaviour. That's one reason some speakers appear as great orators in some countries and in other cultures as raving maniacs.'

'I assume', added David, 'that cultural things like race, religion, beliefs and behaviour influence how messages are received.'

'That's correct. And perceived.' Demosthenes continued scribbling. 'So what may be distracting before one audience may mean something else to another. Now there's another factor that affects perception. It's body language.' He pointed his finger at his young listener.

David crossed his arms. 'I was going to say that.'

'You're being defensive', said Demosthenes.

'No, I'm not', snapped David.

'Yes, you are.'

'I said I'm not', growled David in a louder voice and then gritted his teeth.

'Okay, you're not', said Demosthenes. He laughed. 'I was just proving a point.'

'And that is?'

'That the presenter can use body language that affects perception. You perceived my action as aggressive. Pointing my finger at you caused you to become a little defensive. You have to admit it.'

David nodded as he uncrossed his arms. 'Yeah, I guess I did perceive it as a negative action and was a little defensive. I don't know why but I did. I suppose it was my subconscious at work.'

'That's the power of body language. You see, eighty per cent or more of our communication is through body language. And if you say one thing and the listener sees body language that communicates something different, effective communication becomes difficult, if not impossible. Conflicting messages are conveyed.' Demosthenes spat a pebble into the spittoon. 'Never underestimate the power of body language.'

'So synchronize your body language with what you say', noted David.

'That's right. Now let's talk about language and the meaning of its words.'

'Semantics?' David asked.

'Exactly', said Demosthenes, flipping to the next page. 'Semantics deals with the meaning of words. And we all know that words can have different meanings to different people and that affects the way messages are sent, received and understood. Can you guess some of the more common problems with words?'

David rubbed his chin as he tried to guess the answers. 'Well for one, words can be misinterpreted. Words can evoke negative reactions, even negative actions.'

Demosthenes wrote as David continued. 'They can stereotype or mislead people or misclassify people, places or things.'

'What's the effect of this?'

'It can polarize people, which only builds walls, not bridges, between them', said David.

'Very good, *poulaki mou*', Demosthenes said as he scribbled. 'Very nice symbolism. I like that comparison with walls and bridges. Of course, the goal is to build bridges. So what are some ways to avoid building walls?'

'I'd say, for one, avoid vulgarity', said David.

'Not a bad idea. What else?'

'Avoid slang.'

'And?'

'Try to stay away, I guess, from words related to religion, race and sexism.'

'Excellent. You are politically correct. So now, we need to discuss two more factors that affect perception. The next one is poor listening skills.'

'Yeah, poor listeners really bug me', said David.

'They bug almost everybody, yet, ironically, most people are poor listeners! So what are some behaviours of poor listeners ... ?'

'Interrupting the speaker', said David with a big smirk.

'Cute. But that's one good point. Another?'

'Changing topics in the middle of a ... '

'Another good one', said Demosthenes scribbling. 'And don't forget looking around everywhere but at the person doing the talking.'

'Yeah', agreed David. 'I've had conversations with people who watch other people doing something at the other side of the room, go and pour themselves a cup of coffee, turn up the radio, turn on the television or read a paper while you talk. That really makes me mad.'

'Why?'

'It shows that they don't feel what you say has much importance to them.' David took a deep breath. 'So what can you do to show you're a good listener?'

'One, you can maintain eye contact with the person speaking. Two, you can give some signals that you're listening, either through words, like "yes" or "I understand what you say", or through body language signals, like nodding your head. Three, you let the person finish talking before you say anything. In other words, don't interrupt. Four, you give individual attention to the person talking by not answering the telephone or reading the paper, and things like that. Five, you can paraphrase or rephrase what a person said and ask for affirmation. In short, use much of what you learned on how to handle questions effectively.'

'I hear you', said David, chuckling.

'You're really coming up with cute ones', said Demosthenes. 'But you prove my point that there is a difference between hearing and listening. What is it?'

'With hearing you pick up the noise being made. With listening you understand the noise.' David proudly made a toast and downed his ouzo.

'Obviously, *poulaki mou*, you've been listening', observed Demosthenes. 'So what are the main factors affecting perception of you and your message?'

'Distracting mannerisms', said David, raising a finger for each impediment. 'Semantics ... culture ... body language ... poor listening skills ... unsatisfactory physical environment.' Both hands were upraised. He then lowered them. 'Wow, Demosthenes, I sure am learning good stuff about the communication process. All this really does influence our perception by the audience. It certainly is a complex process. You were right. Earlier, I had only learned the tip of the iceberg.'

Demosthenes nodded. 'That's right, *poulaki mou*, the tip.'

'I want a project that will satisfy their needs', said David. 'And my proposal will do just that. I just have to convince them of that, using their language, terms, beliefs and the like.'

'You're starting to speak like a real pro. I see you've learned a lot already.' The Greek flipped the page. He wrote 'Planning' at the top. 'Now let's discuss planning.'

David felt inspired. 'My strategy is to present my project as a means for satisfying the Board's needs and at the same time contributing greatly to the betterment of mankind, particularly primitive, poor children of the Amazon.'

'Now what tactics will you use?' asked Demosthenes as he wrote.

191

'I've been giving this a lot of thought', said David. 'I think I'll use some slides containing diagrams. At some point, I'd like to use a video or photographic slides as back-up material. I suspect that how I apply these tactics will depend on the psychological impact I want to make.'

'That's correct', said Demosthenes. 'If you employ your tactics to support your strategy, you'll come out a victor. Remember, tactics are the individual actions, main points, or techniques the presenter employs to fulfil the strategy which, in turn, achieves the goals of the presentation.' He spat a pebble into the spittoon. 'Remember?'

David nodded. 'Isn't structure an element in all this?'

'Yes. What about it?'

'Well, I'll stick to the structure with an introduction, discussion and conclusion.'

'Sounds like a smart move to me.' Demosthenes flipped the page and wrote 'Preparation' at the top. 'Ready for the next Pebble of Wisdom?'

'You bet.' David poured himself a shot of ouzo. He looked at the Greek. 'Want some?'

'Not now. I never drink on stage. I'll make a fool of myself and say things I'll regret. I did that once in front of a jury. They thought it was a jug of water but it was filled with wine. Won the case but the next day I had a big headache. I felt as if Zeus had crashed a lightning bolt right on the side of my head. Anyway, let's discuss preparation.'

'Like what?'

'Like *logos*, for one.'

'Yeah', said David. 'I remember. As I said, I'll use the introduction–discussion–conclusion structure. Within that, I can use various structures to present my points, such as problem/solution, time/sequence, simple/complex, question/answer or topical.'

'Excellent', said Demosthenes. 'Excellent memory of our earlier discussions.'

'I'll never forget what I learned from you, Demost. It's all good stuff.'

'Thank you, *poulaki mou*. So that brings us to the next element of preparation ... '

'*Pathos*', snapped David, feeling tipsy from the ouzo.

'That's right. The emotional content of the presentation.' Demosthenes spat a pebble into the spittoon. 'For persuasive presentations, using *pathos* is of paramount importance. I can't overstress its importance.' Demosthenes made a fist and tapped it against his chest as he spoke. 'You have to affect people right here in the heart. That means buttressing your logic and points with examples, statistics, facts and illustrations. But using them and other ploys in such a way as to bring about the desired effect. It's a real art form. And that's exactly what happened when I developed and delivered my Philippics. I really emphasized the *pathos*. I needed to urge the Athenians to action.' The Greek gave a slight cough and then asked, 'Remember the topic of memory?'

'Yeah, I didn't forget', said David with a slur. His head was spinning from the liqueur. 'You wanted to save it for later.'

'Well, now's the time to discuss it. Just to refresh your memory, you might recall that over time, memory declines.'

David nodded, along with his eyelids.

'That happens during and after presentations', said Demosthenes. 'So as a presenter, you need to take certain actions for increasing the audience's memory. What are they?'

'Using good illustrations', snapped David.

'You remember well. But here's one that Socrates, Aristotle and Plato were good at', said Demosthenes, spitting a pebble into the spittoon. 'They used analogies to improve listeners' learning and memory.'

'Sort of like a teacher.'

'Good analogy', said Demosthenes with a chuckle. 'You can also employ certain techniques when you're delivering your presentation. But we'll save those for later.'

'Let's now discuss *ethos*', said the Greek, turning the next page. 'And *ethos* is?'

'The moral or ethical content of a presentation', answered David. 'It has a lot to do with appearing credible.'

'What are some factors that can increase your credibility if used correctly?'

'I'd say how you present yourself', said David. 'Also, reputation plays a role. As I said earlier, it all deals with credibility.'

'I agree. Just as it was for the other presentations.' Demosthenes scribbled his last comment and left the stage. He sat at the table. 'Now, I'd like to discuss the next two Pebbles of Wisdom, practice and performance, in the context of persuasive presentations. But rather than do it here where you could fall asleep from too much ouzo and have your face smash on to the table, I'd like us to discuss them in the park where we first met.' He removed a notebook and pen from his pocket and tossed them towards David. 'And bring these with you.'

David picked up the materials from the table, ran up to the stage, removed the papers from the flipchart and, wobbling close behind, followed the Greek out through the entrance.

# Chapter 35

David gripped the inside door handle as Demosthenes wove the car in and out of the traffic. It seemed that every time he passed another car Demosthenes beeped the horn.

'The people in this city sure don't know how to drive', said the Greek.

David felt himself sobering quickly. 'Yeah. You'd think they'd practise their driving more.' He pressed his shoulder against the door as the car took a sharp turn around the corner. The centrifugal force made his stomach churn.

'It took me a long time to learn how to drive in this kind of traffic.' The Greek zipped in between two large vehicles, a bus and an eighteen-wheel truck. 'They're going far too slow.' Demosthenes beeped his horn as he pulled the car out from between the two vehicles.

David gripped the handrail on the ceiling.

'Nervous?' asked Demosthenes, looking at David.

'Me?' David looked ahead. 'Watch out!'

Demosthenes turned his head and noticed the old lady walking in the road. He sharply turned the steering wheel to bypass the woman. 'Some people just take their time. They think nothing's ever going to happen to them. No foresight. Which brings us to the next Pebble of Wisdom, practice. The best foresight for presentations is to practise. You might want to take notes.'

David reached into his shirt pocket and removed the notebook and pen. He started to write.

'All that we talked about with regard to practice for informative and explanatory presentations applies', continued the Greek, 'to persuasive presentations. But there are some additions. Are you writing?' he asked, turning his head.

David nodded but was too terrified to speak. The numbness in his face was now from fear, not ouzo.

'Good', said Demosthenes, looking again at the road. 'In your practice sessions you need to concentrate on the psychological impact of your presentation. Ask yourself this question: "Would I be convinced of what I'm saying?" If you can't say yes, you'll have to go back to the drawing board. Still writing all this down?'

David nodded his head up and down repeatedly and said in a high-pitched voice, 'Yes.'

'You sound nervous, David. Make sure you work on your nervousness during practice sessions.'

'I will', said David in a high pitch. 'I will.'

'Very good.' Demosthenes swerved around a car. 'Here are some additional clues for good practice sessions to control nervousness.'

'I'm writing', David said as the car slammed to a halt at a red light.

'Try to make where you rehearse resemble as much as possible the environment where you'll give the final presentation.' The light turned green and Demosthenes pressed his foot on the accelerator.

David's back smacked against the seat as the car lunged forward.

'And', continued Demosthenes, 'try to visualize how you want the presentation to go. Do that two or three times and then practise. Visualize it from the moment you first walk through the doors of the room.'

The car entered a parking lot and came to a screeching halt. Demosthenes turned off the ignition. 'Do you have any questions?'

'Yeah', said David, after taking a deep breath. 'Where did you learn to drive?'

'Athens', said Demosthenes. 'Why?'

# Chapter 36

'Why are we here?' asked David as he followed Demosthenes towards a small crowd assembled around a man speaking to them.

'There's a political rally going on here in the park, today. You'll find plenty of real examples of good and poor persuasive presentations.' Demosthenes chose a small bench and sat down. 'This is a good place to listen to that fellow.' He pointed to a man standing before the crowd.

David sat next to Demosthenes, and they listened for five minutes.

'Well', observed David, 'this guy's no dynamo. He's about as exciting as a corpse.'

'True', said Demosthenes, nodding. 'So what else did you observe?'

David cleared his throat. 'He's not displaying much enthusiasm. His face is expressionless. He's using no gestures. And he shouts out a bunch of boring statistics.'

'Good observations. What else?'

'He's speaking in a monotonous voice. And he's not maintaining eye contact with the audience. He keeps looking over the audience's heads. In fact, he makes it so obvious that he seems to be looking even over our heads.'

'Now you know some things not to do', said Demosthenes. 'Now start taking notes.'

David removed his notebook and pencil from his shirt pocket and sat ready to write. 'Ready, Demost.'

Demosthenes reached into his pocket, removed some pebbles and tossed them into his mouth. He spat one on to the ground.

'First and foremost, *poulaki mou*, show some enthusiasm. Communicate to the audience through body language that you want to be in front of them. What are some things you can do to accomplish that?'

'Ah', said David, as he scribbled, 'you can maintain eye contact with the audience.'

'Good. What else?'

'You can gesture more but in a way that is natural', said David.

'Keep writing', Demosthenes said, spitting a pebble. 'There's more.'

'You can also smile.'

'Excellent. The guy up there speaking should be listening to you. There's one subject that we're mentioning but not enough. It has something to do with the vocal chords.'

'Your voice', David said.

'Exactly. You can use your voice like the sirens, who sang to attract sailors and drive them mad with desire. You may not be as melodious as them but you can use your voice to your advantage. You can use it to communicate enthusiasm and emphasize significant points in your presentation. But let's talk first about using your voice to show enthusiasm.'

'Okay', David said, ready to record the Greek's thoughts.

'You can increase your volume. However, it's best to be conversational and increase volume only at certain times during the presentation.'

David scribbled.

'You can increase the rate or pace. But strive to talk at a moderate rate, which is anywhere from 125 to 160 words per minute. Are you noting this down?'

'Yeah', David said.

'Good. Now, as for pitch, be normal. From time to time you may want to change the pitch to draw attention to a point.'

'So basically', said David, 'you want to be as natural as possible but use variety when necessary.' He scribbled as he talked.

'Excellent. You know, David, you're sounding more and more like a professional.'

David smiled. 'Thanks.'

'But don't get overconfident', said Demosthenes, pointing his finger skyward. 'There's more to master.'

'Like what?'

'Well, you see all these people standing around? They're reading papers. Talking among themselves. Almost ignoring the poor guy. We need to find what you call a dynamo. Let's go.'

David rose from the bench and followed the Greek to another group. Only this time, the speaker stood on his bench. Both entered into the crowd and listened for a few minutes. The audience was soon yelling at the speaker. People were throwing fruit and paper at him.

'Well, this is a first. In almost twenty-five hundred years, I've never seen a speaker alienate an audience so fast', said Demosthenes.

'Yeah, he turned the audience on. On himself', said David, nervously. 'Maybe we should go.'

'Not yet', said Demosthenes. 'There are some good lessons here. Ready to take notes?'

'Yeah', said David with the notebook and pen in hand. 'Go ahead.'

'Besides being pompous and arrogant, what else was he?'

'Ridiculing and insulting. And his use of sarcasm certainly did not endear him to the audience.'

200

'Exactly. Anything else?'

'His humour didn't seem very funny. As soon as he had finished his joke, I knew things would be flying', said David, chuckling.

'You're laughing', snapped Demosthenes who then spat a pebble. 'But humour has to be handled very carefully. Make sure you're positive, not negative. I suggest you stay away from religious, political and ethnic humour. Sex is a taboo, too. That builds, as you say, walls and not bridges. Humour should also be related to the presentation, not overshadow the main objective. And be brief.'

'You know, Demost, this reminds me of a good one', David said, writing. 'Have you heard ... ?'

'No, and I don't think this is the time to tell a joke. Things are getting pretty tense here. He's angered just about everyone, probably even Zeus', said Demosthenes, looking skyward. 'I wouldn't be surprised if Zeus hurled an angry thunderbolt any second. Come on, let's go and look for an example of a good presentation.'

David and Demosthenes ambled for some distance until they noticed dozens of people listening to a young man. The listeners were applauding vigorously.

'This looks like a good one', said the Greek, leading the way through the crowd. He and David stood listening to the speech for several minutes.

'This guy's great', whispered David. He turned to look behind him. The size of the audience had almost doubled.

'That's my observation, too', said Demosthenes. He spat a pebble on to the ground. 'Notebook and pen ready?'

'Yeah', said David, waiting to take notes.

'Good.' Demosthenes pointed to the speaker. 'Brilliant. Look how that man communicates. He does it well, don't you think?'

'Sure does', whispered David. He prepared to take notes.

'What about his physical behaviour?' asked Demosthenes, spitting a pebble. 'Like his gestures.'

'He used gestures to support his main ideas', observed David, writing. 'They seemed natural, not forced. He seemed to time them well. They were "in sync" with what he said.'

'And his voice?'

'His voice was conversational and seemed synchronized with his message', said David. 'He raised and lowered the volume to emphasize different points. His articulation was clear. And what was interesting was that he varied the pace to emphasize a point. He even paused at certain times to build suspense before making his point. All in all, good vocal variety.'

'And his body movements?'

'Great. Like his gestures, he used the same facial expressions to emphasize a point. You could see pleasure and displeasure clearly when he made a point.'

'What do you think about his jumping down from the bench and mingling with the crowd as he spoke?'

'Great', said David, scribbling while his hand grew tired. 'He didn't treat the bench as a pulpit to scream to his audience. He left the bench to talk with his audience. Nice touch, I thought.'

'And what about eye contact?'

'He kept it through the entire speech. At times I felt as if he was talking only to me.'

'Did you like the way he related to the audience?'

David nodded as he continued to write. 'Yeah. He showed enthusiasm. And he wasn't arrogant, condescending, pompous, insulting or sarcastic. He used few statistics and the ones he did use he rounded off rather than mention a series of numbers with decimal points.'

'Is that all?' asked Demosthenes, spitting a pebble.

'Not only did he keep the statistics simple; he used simple language. No jargon or high-falutin' words. I also noticed that he repeated ideas and words. They seem to ring again in the back of my mind.' He continued scribbling.

'Did you notice that he did something that I had forgotten completely about?' asked Demosthenes.

'I ... ah ... I don't know', said David.

'Write this down', ordered the Greek. 'He received audience involvement by asking questions!'

'Yeah', said David. 'That certainly did engage the audience's attention and involvement.'

'An old trick, but an effective one', said Demosthenes. 'It can be an actual question for the audience to answer or one that begs the question. Right?'

'Huh?' asked David, preoccupied with writing. 'Oh yeah. Right.'

'It's late', said Demosthenes. 'It's time to call it a day.'

David followed the Greek to the car. 'Gosh, Demosthenes, I've learned a lot of good stuff from you.'

'There's still a few more points to discuss. Jump in the car and I'll tell you while I take you back to your apartment.'

David climbed into the car. The confidence he had just acquired soon disappeared as the car jerked backwards.

'Now let's talk just a little bit more about presentations. Are you taking notes?' asked the Greek as he rolled down the window and spat a pebble.

'Yeah', said David in a nervous voice.

'Good.' Demosthenes stepped on the accelerator as he turned down a long narrow street leading to a main road. 'Let's discuss the time of day for giving presentations. We discussed it briefly earlier.'

'Okay', said David, gripping the handrail on the ceiling of the car. His left hand wrote on the notepad resting on his left knee.

'When do you think is the worst time to give presentations?'

'During a car ride?' asked David, finding it hard to concentrate or write. His eyes were riveted to the front.

'I'll tell you then', said Demosthenes, releasing the clutch and making the car lunge forward. As the car moved on, he took one hand off the wheel, pointed, and talked. 'Try to avoid giving presentations on Mondays and Fridays. Why?'

'Ah … ' David found it hard to think and write as the car wove in and out between other vehicles. 'I know', he said in a soft voice. 'Because on Mondays and Fridays people think about other things like going back to work or getting ready to leave it.'

'Exactly, *poulaki mou*.' Demosthenes turned and asked: 'What about afternoons, especially after lunches?'

'A real presentation killer. The reason is that their bodies are thinking about digesting food, not information. And watch out for that truck!'

'But if you have to give presentations at those times', continued Demosthenes, 'be sure to concentrate on keeping the audience's attention. Any ideas?'

'Yeah. You can involve the audience in the presentation', said David.

'Good. What actions can you take to make that happen?'

'I can ask the audience questions', said David. 'I can also give demonstrations that a member or even members of the audience participate in.'

'Good. What other types of actions can you take?'

'Well', David said as he rubbed his chin, 'I can give more frequent breaks … Make sure the temperature and lighting are comfortable … '

'What about yourself?'

'I could gesture more … Use more vocal variety … Walk into the audience.'

Demosthenes slammed on the brake. 'That guy's red lights weren't working.' He beeped the horn. 'Anyway, *poulaki mou*, that leads to the next question. When is it a good time to give presentations if you have a choice?'

'By a process of elimination, I'd say the mornings of Tuesday, Wednesday or Thursday.'

Demosthenes stepped on the accelerator. 'Exactly.' He turned the corner sharply. 'Now let's talk about the configuration of the room where you'll give your presentation.'

'Sounds good to me', said David. His throat became dry.

'Now take good notes', said the Greek. 'This is important.'

'I am, I am.' David felt the centrifugal force press his shoulder against the car door.

'Good. What should you look for with regard to lighting?'

'Whether it's too dark or too bright', David said, scribbling.

'And the equipment?'

'Whether it's the right equipment and if it works.'

'And the supplies?'

'Whether the right supplies are available and in the right quantities.'

'And the temperature, David?'

'Whether it is too hot or cold.'

'And the spacing?'

'Whether the seating is crammed or the room's too big.'

'Any more?'

'Whether acoustics are fine and there's little interference from outside noise.'

'Don't forget', said Demosthenes, 'consider the sound system. That can affect acoustics and the size of the room and its contents can also affect them dramatically.'

'Yeah.' David watched straight ahead as Demosthenes zoomed past a red light. 'You just passed through a red light.'

'I did that to prove a point.'

'Oh?' David asked. 'What's that?' He heart pounded. His forehead began to sweat even more. His blood raced. One of his eyelids twitched. All the symptoms, he thought, of stage fright.

'You need', said Demosthenes, 'to arrive early to check all this. Or at least some time before the presentation. Determining all this at the time of the presentation would be too late.'

David scribbled the last of the notes as the car screeched to a halt. He turned and looked out the window. He let out a sigh of relief.

'Well, *poulaki mou*, you're back at your apartment block.'

'Care to come up?' asked David as he quickly opened the door and leaped outside.

'Would very much like to. But I'm taking someone special out to dinner tonight.'

'Really?' David asked. 'Who?'

The Greek pointed over David's shoulder.

'Mom!' said David, feeling his jaw dropping open and looking at a woman dressed as if for a formal ball.

'Hi son', she said, climbing into the car.

'Bye, mom', he said, closing the car door for her.

He stood silent as he watched the car disappear down the street.

# Chapter 37

The moment of truth had arrived. David opened the large mahogany doors to the conference room.

Arriving at this point in time had not been easy. He had worked long hours, from the early mornings into the late evenings, building his presentation and practising the delivery. He had even managed to go inside the conference room earlier to see what was available. If practice makes perfect, he was now perfectly ready to give the presentation.

Or so he thought. As he stepped into the room, he noticed nine staid, conservatively dressed people turning their heads and staring at him from a long oval, mahogany table. He recognized one of them from his earlier days, Craig Yuggenheim, chairman and president of the Yuggenheim Corporation. Craig, a heavy-set man, wore a dark grey suit and a maroon tie. He rose from his chair and approached David.

They shook hands.

'Welcome', said Craig. He guided David towards the other side of the conference table. Craig introduced David to the others.

David proceeded to the podium that stood at the very end of the conference room. Behind the podium were two large screens, one on the left and the other on the right. Next to the podium was an overhead projector on a small stand and on the opposite side was a video cassette machine that was connected to the large television in the right corner of the room. Next to the video cassette machine was a slide projector. His first slide was still in place on the platen of the overhead projector. The handouts rested on the shelf inside the podium and the remaining slides were in a binder on the table of the overhead projector but hidden from the audience.

Everything, just as he had requested, was in place and ready. Good planning had paid off. Minimum effort and distraction now, thanks to coordinating earlier with the secretary.

David felt a sudden rush of excitement overcome him. His heart pounded. His palms became moist. His temples throbbed. And butterflies came to his stomach.

But he did not panic. He recognized the symptoms for what they were – nervousness, the energy that would communicate enthusiasm to the audience. He smiled gently as he maintained eye contact with the audience.

Then he noticed something that almost paralysed him. My God, he thought.

Demosthenes was nowhere in the room, at least not visibly.

Where are you, Demost? he thought. You said you were going to be here! His eyes scanned the room. There were no windows so Demosthenes could not hang outside. There were no cupboards for him to hide in. The temperature in the room was perfect so no maintenance help was necessary. Everything was in its place.

Except Demost.

He must be somewhere, David thought repeatedly in an effort to reassure himself. Maybe he's hiding under the conference table or above the hanging ceiling. Yeah, that's it. The old Greek is a tricky one!

David released a gentle sigh and hit the button on the overhead projector, revealing an image that was focused, just as he had tested yesterday.

---

### *YUGGENHEIM FOUNDATION*

### LOVE IS FOR EVERYONE PROPOSAL

---

### LOVE IS FOR EVERYONE PROPOSAL


### David Michaels

### November 3, 19XX

---

'Good morning ladies and gentlemen', he said in a conversational tone while standing, not leaning, on the podium. 'As we are all aware, my topic is to present to you my proposal on ... ' He paused for a second and looked at everyone directly in the eye and then continued, 'the Love Is For Everyone project. Or LIFE project for short.'

He removed the slide and placed a new one on the platen.

```
┌─────────────────────────────────────────────┐
│                                               │
│         YUGGENHEIM FOUNDATION                 │
│                                               │
│                                               │
│      LOVE IS FOR EVERYONE PROPOSAL            │
│                                               │
├───────────────────────────────────────────────┤
│                                               │
│                  AGENDA                       │
│                                               │
│                                               │
│        ☞   Introduction                       │
│                                               │
│        ☞   Background                         │
│                                               │
│        ☞   Proposal                           │
│                                               │
│        ☞   Description                        │
│                                               │
│        ☞   Business Case                      │
│                                               │
│        ☞   Conclusion                         │
│                                               │
│        ☞   Next Steps                         │
│                                               │
│                                               │
└───────────────────────────────────────────────┘
```

'But before I launch into the details of my proposal, I would like to share with you the agenda of my presentation.' He did just that and told them they could ask questions at any time.

He proceeded to show the next slide.

**YUGGENHEIM FOUNDATION**

**LOVE IS FOR EVERYONE PROPOSAL**

---

**INTRODUCTION**

PURPOSE

Set up hospital facility
site and hospital ship
to traverse the Amazon
Basin

'As you can see here', he said, as he moved from the podium and took some steps towards the audience, making sure that he wasn't blocking the image, 'the purpose of the LIFE project is to establish a hospital facility and ship in the Amazon region, often referred to as Amazonia.'

He returned to the podium and showed the next slide.

'I would like to limit the project to providing healthcare services to the at-risk and underprivileged children in the Amazon region.'

David turned off the overhead projector. 'I managed to contact the Red Cross and they were able to provide me with a videotape on the conditions of the millions of poor children in the Amazon Basin. It takes about five minutes but I think you'll appreciate the need for what the LIFE project will achieve.'

He dimmed the lights of the room from the control panel at the podium and turned on the video cassette player. After it was finished, he stopped the tape and slowly increased the intensity of the lights. He returned to the podium.

David noticed that everyone's staid look was replaced with a sullen one. He saw that he had touched their hearts in addition to their heads.

Except for one. David noticed that the man had crossed his arms over his chest and had a smirk on his face.

David asked if there were any questions or comments and paused for a second. The man in the defensive posture raised his hand.

'Yes, sir', said David, concentrating on not communicating any defensive body language.

'You do a good job of telling us about the poverty of Amazonia and the need for your project but the Yuggenheim Foundation can't save the world.'

David paused for a second or two before responding, formulating his answer and ensuring that it did not increase the man's defensiveness. He stepped from the podium and moved towards the questioner. 'Your point is well taken. But the Yuggenheim Foundation can play an instrumental role in changing the lives of a substantial number of people, even though it may not change the world.'

'I agree with Mr Michaels', said another Board member. 'Something like this won't alter the world dramatically but it will make the world a better place to live in for some.'

'Are there any other questions or comments?' asked David. He waited a few seconds but, seeing no hands and hearing no voices, he returned to the podium.

He showed the next slide.

## *YUGGENHEIM FOUNDATION*

## LOVE IS FOR EVERYONE PROPOSAL

### BACKGROUND

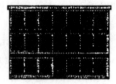   

☞  Hospital Facility
- Three levels
- Full-scale services
- Fixed location

☞  Hospital Ship
- Three levels
- Smaller-scale
  services
- Remote sites

'I understand that the Executive Steering Committee submitted a report to you before this meeting. Therefore, I'll just briefly describe what the hospital facility will consist of.'

He gave the overview of the hospital facility and ship and changed to the next slide.

'To date, the LIFE proposal has been approved by two internal bodies of the Yuggenheim Foundation, the New Projects Council and the Executive Steering Committee. They, of course, have received a more detailed presentation of what the facility and ship will be like. My understanding is that this Board concerns itself with the business case which I will present if there are no further questions.'

He paused for a few seconds and showed the next slide.

---

### YUGGENHEIM FOUNDATION

### LOVE IS FOR EVERYONE PROPOSAL

---

## BUSINESS CASE

☞ People

☞ Materials/Supplies

☞ Equipment/Machinery

☞ Facilities

☞ Financial Analysis

☞ Risk Management

☞ Schedule

---

'In preparing the business case, I looked at a number of factors.'
He turned and pointed at the list and then faced the audience.
'I would like to discuss each one.'

He showed the next slide.

216

**BUSINESS CASE**

People

| PEOPLE | HOSPITAL FACILITY | HOSPITAL SHIP |
|---|---|---|
| Medical staff | X | X |
| Speciality areas | X | X |
| Administrative personnel | X | X |
| Maintenance staff | X | X |
| Ship crew | | X |

'As you can see here', said David, removing his pointer from his shirt pocket and extending it, 'a number of people will be required to make the LIFE project a reality.' He pointed to the empty cell under Hospital Facility. 'Of course,' he said, as he ensured he was talking to the audience and not to the screen, 'you see that a ship's crew is not necessary for the facility.'

He showed the next slide.

## YUGGENHEIM FOUNDATION

## LOVE IS FOR EVERYONE PROPOSAL

## BUSINESS CASE

### Materials/Supplies

| MATERIALS/SUPPLIES | HOSPITAL FACILITY | HOSPITAL SHIP |
|---|---|---|
| General hospital items | X | X |
| Specialized hospital items | X | X |
| Administrative items | X | X |
| Spare parts | | X |

'A number of materials and supplies will be required', he said, making sure not to play with the pointer and holding it steady in his hand.

A Board member raised her hand. 'Are there hard numbers for the chart where you have Xs?'

David nodded as he closed the pointer and placed it in his shirt. 'Yes. The handout that I shall distribute after the presentation will contain a detailed listing for your review. In the financial analysis which will be covered later, I will be presenting some aggregate figures. Any further questions?'

Hearing and seeing no indication, he presented the next slide.

## YUGGENHEIM FOUNDATION

## LOVE IS FOR EVERYONE PROPOSAL

### BUSINESS CASE

Equipment/Machinery

| EQUIPMENT/MACHINERY | HOSPITAL FACILITY | HOSPITAL SHIP |
|---|:---:|:---:|
| General equipment/ machinery | X | X |
| Fixed hospital equipment/ machinery | X | X |
| Movable hospital equipment/machinery | X | X |
| Spare parts | | X |

'Equipment and machinery will also be needed.'
He showed the next slide.

'And naturally facilities will be needed during construction. Now for the key question. What will all this cost?' he asked as he raised the volume of his voice. He noticed some of the Board members shifted in their chairs while others raised their eyebrows. None, he noticed, sat defensively.

He showed the next slide.

220

---

**YUGGENHEIM FOUNDATION**

**LOVE IS FOR EVERYONE PROPOSAL**

---

**BUSINESS CASE**

Financial Analysis

Start-up cost in $m* (in today's dollars)

| | | |
|---|---|---|
| People | | 10 |
| Materials/Supplies | | 5 |
| Equipment/Machinery | | 30 |
| Facilities | | 40 |
| | Total | 85 |

*Includes both Hospital Facility and Hospital Ship

---

'The total cost, as you can see here, ladies and gentlemen,' continued David as he removed his pointer and extended it, indicated the total and increased the volume of his voice, 'is roughly eighty-five million dollars.'

David paused for several seconds, letting the Board members study the figure and giving them an opportunity to formulate any questions or comments.

A Board member spoke in a low voice. 'Does this figure account for any contingencies?'

221

David repeated the question and said, 'Yes sir. The figure that everyone sees accounts for contingencies, for all categories shown here, and for maintenance and operational costs.'

He walked to the overhead projector, being sure not to play with the pointer, and showed the next slide.

---

### *YUGGENHEIM FOUNDATION*

### LOVE IS FOR EVERYONE PROPOSAL

---

### BUSINESS CASE

Financial Analysis

Maintenance cost per year in $m
(in today's dollars)*

| | |
|---|---|
| People | 10 |
| Materials/Supplies | 2 |
| Equipment/Machinery | 4 |
| Facilities | 2 |
| Total | 18 |

*Includes both Hospital Facility and Hospital Ship

---

He returned to the screen, not blocking the image and continuing to face the audience. He pointed to the total. 'The maintenance and operational costs come to eighteen million per annum.' He showed the next slide after giving them time to study the figures.

---

### YUGGENHEIM FOUNDATION

### LOVE IS FOR EVERYONE PROPOSAL

---

### BUSINESS CASE

Financial Analysis

- Tax write-off     →   $35 m (in today's dollars)

- Net present value   →   $60 m (in today's dollars)

- Internal rate of return   →   25%

- Payback period   →   4 years

Note: The above figures include both Hospital Facility and Hospital Ship

---

'The payback, shown here, is considerable, even if this is a non-profit organization. Notice that the Yuggenheim Corporation will have a substantial write-off and an attractive return on invest-ment to finance other charitable causes.'

'What about the risks? The figures look quite impressive but there are risks', said the same Board member who commented earlier about trying to save the world. He crossed his arms again and smirked.

'I agree', said David, putting his pointer away in his shirt pocket and approaching the overhead projector. 'That brings me to the next point.' David noticed that the man uncrossed his arms. He changed the slide.

---

### YUGGENHEIM FOUNDATION

### LOVE IS FOR EVERYONE PROPOSAL

---

### BUSINESS CASE

Risk Management

- Risk Assessment is Medium to High
  – Based on broad scope of requirements

- Risk Abatement
  – Appoint senior programme manager
  – Hold monthly checkpoint reviews

---

'At this juncture, I assess the risks as anywhere from medium to high. A significant contributing factor to this risk is acquiring the personnel with the right expertise to build and maintain both the facility and ship. But', continued David as he paused to draw attention to his forthcoming comments, 'the best abatement plan is to appoint a highly qualified programme manager who will hold regular reviews with the Board as to status.'

'And what is the timescale for this project?' asked another Board member.

'That leads me to my next point', David said. 'Thank you for the cue.' The audience chuckled.

He displayed the next slide.

---

## YUGGENHEIM FOUNDATION

### LOVE IS FOR EVERYONE PROPOSAL

---

### START-UP SCHEDULE

#### Summary

| | Months | | | | | | | | | | | | | | | | | |
|---|---|---|---|---|---|---|---|---|---|---|---|---|---|---|---|---|---|---|
| | 1 | 2 | 3 | 4 | 5 | 6 | 7 | 8 | 9 | 10 | 11 | 12 | 13 | 14 | 15 | 16 | 17 | 18 |
| People | | | | | | | | | | | | | | | | | | |
| Materials/Supplies | | | | | | | | | | | | | | | | | | |
| Equipment/ Machinery | | | | | | | | | | | | | | | | | | |
| Facilities | | | | | | | | | | | | | | | | | | |

Note: The above schedule includes both Hospital Facility and Hospital Ship

---

'Basically, the project will take eighteen months to complete. That's for the facility and ship.'
David showed the next slide.

---

### YUGGENHEIM FOUNDATION

### LOVE IS FOR EVERYONE PROPOSAL

---

### CONCLUSION

☞ Amazon River Basin
- Size of the continental USA
- Population is 11 million people

☞ Health
- 40% live without proper sanitation
- 30% are malnourished
- 10% of children are abandoned

---

'I'd like to say that the Amazon Basin is a big place. Few people know much about it despite its size in terms of land and population.' He returned to the podium. He pressed a button activating the photographic slide projector. An image of a little Indian girl in tattered pink clothes and a face splattered with mud appeared on the screen.

'The little girl shown here', said David, pointing to the photographic slide, 'is reflected in those statistics shown here', pointing to the figures on the overhead projection. He paused for a second, ensuring that the image of the little girl was firmly planted in their minds.

He showed the next slide.

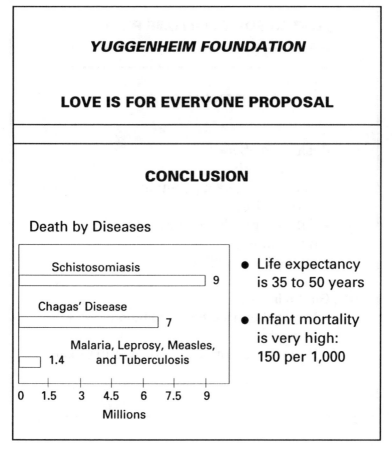

'And', he said, raising the volume of his voice, 'she, like the others, will face death from diseases like these, whether as an infant or at an age we consider the prime of our lives.'

He left the slide up for a few seconds and then displayed the next one.

---

**YUGGENHEIM FOUNDATION**

**LOVE IS FOR EVERYONE PROPOSAL**

---

**CONCLUSION**

☞ Positive Payback
 – Tax write-off
 – Improved market penetration for products and services
 – Futures for joint venture with foreign government
 – Intangible benefits

☞ Global Impact
 – Yuggenheim's are first to help world's last frontier
 – Promotes spirituality and hope in today's world

---

'But please keep in mind that not only do little girls and boys benefit, like the little girl shown here,' said David as he pointed to her image and then at the slide, 'so do the Yuggenheim Foundation

and all mankind in general for the reasons I have listed here.' He
gave them a few seconds to look at the list.
He then showed the last slide.

---

### YUGGENHEIM FOUNDATION

### LOVE IS FOR EVERYONE PROPOSAL

---

### NEXT STEPS

☞ Receive approval from Board of
Directors

☞ Assign Programme Manager

☞ Obtain funding

---

'So what's next?' asked David, as he made a concerted effort to
look everyone in the eyes. He noticed that they were focused
directly on him, too. 'First,' he said, raising the index finger on his
right hand, 'approval is necessary from you, ladies and gentlemen.' He raised a second finger, keeping the last one up. 'Two, the
Board needs to assign a programme manager. And third,' he con-

229

tinued as he jutted up a third finger, holding his hand up, 'the Board must authorize the necessary funding.'

David turned off the overhead projector but not the slide projector. The image of the little girl remained on the screen.

'Are there any questions or comments?' he asked as he took the handouts off the shelf inside the podium.

Craig Yuggenheim spoke after several long seconds of silence. 'We shall make our decision within the next ten minutes. Could you please take a seat in the lobby as we deliberate? We shall have the secretary call you in when we have decided.'

'Yes sir', said David as he distributed the handouts. He left the conference room and walked down the hallway. God, it's in your hands, he thought. I've done the best I ... What? He squinted his eyes. 'It can't be', he said to himself. 'No, it can't.' He became weak. His stomach became agitated. He sat down on one of the hallway chairs as he waited for the all too familiar face to come closer. 'Demost ... '

'David!' he said. 'I'm sorry I'm late. Is the presentation over?'

'I thought you were in there. I thought you were either in the ceiling or under the table. Why weren't you there?'

'Breakfast took a little longer than I anticipated', said the Greek, placing his hand on David's shoulder. 'And the roads were really congested. Sorry, *poulaki mou*.'

'Breakfast? You were at breakfast while I gave the most important presentation of my life?'

'Yes, son. A very important breakfast, I might add.'

David gave Demosthenes a strange look. 'Son?'

'Yes. Son.' The Greek took a chair and placed it next to David's. 'That's right. Son. Your mother and I have decided to get married.'

'Get what?' said David. The agitation in his stomach was turning to nausea. 'Married? I don't understand.'

'Listen, David. Your mother and I have discussed this at great length. That's why I failed to be here on time. Looking for a woman like your mother took me close to twenty-five hundred years.'

'You sure you're not rushing into things?' David asked in a sarcastic tone, followed by a nervous laugh.

'Without a doubt, son. Without a … '

The secretary interrupted the conversation while looking at Demosthenes suspiciously. 'Mr Michaels. The Board has made its decision.'

David rose from his chair as he stared at Demosthenes.

'Good luck … son,' said the Greek, followed by a smile.

I'm going to the firing squad, thought David. First, Demosthenes tells me that we'll be father and son. Now I'll be rejected by the Board. Oh well, I might as well be very Greek and accept my fate.

The secretary opened the door. As David followed her into the room, everyone rose from their chairs and applauded.

'Congratulations', said Craig Yuggenheim, extending his arm. They shook hands vigorously. 'The Board has approved your proposal and would like you to be the programme manager. That was a very good presentation. The best this Board's ever seen.'

David turned towards the entrance of the conference room. He noticed Demosthenes standing in the doorway, expressionless.

'And who might that fellow be?' asked Craig.

'That man … ' said David followed by a big sigh, 'that man is my dad.'

He watched as the biggest grin planted itself on the Greek's face.

# Chapter 38

Three hundred-plus people milled about the lounge occasionally selecting ambrosia from the queue of tables running opposite the stage. By anyone's standards, the wedding reception was going well.

Demetri climbed on to the stage and yelled for everyone's attention. The band playing *demotiki* lowered their instruments. The folk dancers stopped doing the *kalamatiano*[1] and walked down the stage steps. 'Gals and gents', he said amidst some grumbling. 'Our Mr Michaels here is gonna tell ya something. So listen up.' He stepped off the stage.

David climbed on to the stage. He stood silent for a second, working on controlling the nervous energy that comes to anyone standing before such a large crowd. In his hand was a glass of champagne; the right side of his cheek bulged ...

'Friends. Today is a big moment in my life and in the life of my mom. The reason is a very special person is now a member of my family.'

---

[1]*Kalamatiano*: the national dance of Greece where everyone holds hands.

He walked about the stage and gestured with his one free hand. 'This man has taught me so much good stuff about giving effective presentations in such a short period of time that I can face a crowd as large as this one with confidence.

'He's revealed to me six great Pebbles of Wisdom that I feel I must share with you on this happy occasion.' David pointed one finger skyward as he spat a pebble into his champagne glass. 'First, there's perspective … knowing yourself and your listeners. It's the same when two people meet. Each one learns as much as possible about the other. Like mom and Demost.'

Chuckling came from the audience. He spat another pebble.

'Second,' he said as he raised a second finger, 'there's perception … how you perceive people and how they, in turn, perceive you. Like how two people perceive each other when they first meet. Just like mom and Demost.'

More chuckling. Another pebble came from his mouth.

'Third,' he continued as he raised a third finger, 'there's planning.' David walked around the stage. 'You determine the strategy and tactics to get from point A to point Z. It's similar to determining how to approach building a solid relationship with another person. Like mom and Demost.'

Still more chuckling. He spat another pebble.

'Fourth,' he said as another finger shot upward, 'there's preparation … laying the groundwork on which to build the presentation so that your strategy and tactics become reality. It's like doing the right things to please the other person. Just like mom and Demost.'

Even more chuckling.

'Fifth,' he said as he raised another finger and spat a pebble, 'there's practice … doing whatever you have to do to perfect your presentation. It's like getting ready for a big date. You practise communicating well with your partner to build a meaningful relationship. Just like mom and Demost.'

The chuckling turned to laughter.

'Sixth,' he said, as he kept all five fingers raised, lifted skyward the champagne glass to represent the sixth point and spat a pebble, 'there's performance ... the moment of truth. You have to communicate effectively. Just like mom and ... dad.'

The laughter turned into applause.

He raised the champagne glass even higher into the air as he looked at his mom and Demosthenes standing together with their arms around each other. Then he shouted with a flattened cheek, 'Chronia polla!'[1]

---

[1]Chronia polla: 'many years', a phrase wishing good luck.

# CHECKLISTS

# INTRODUCTION

Keeping in mind Demosthenes'
six Pebbles of Wisdom (POW),
use the following checklists to help
you give winning presentations. You
can start at any of the six POWs.

<u>No.</u>

|   |   |   |
|---|---|---|
| ● | Types of Presentation | 1 |
| ① | Perspective | 2 |
| ② | Perception | 3 |
| ③ | Planning | 4–5 |
| ④ | Preparation | 6–17 |
| ⑤ | Practice | 18–20 |
| ⑥ | Performance | 21–41 |

237

## TYPES OF PRESENTATION

☐ Informative – conveys or communicates information

☐ Explanatory – provides an understanding of how something works or occurs

☐ Persuasive – convinces the audience to your way of thinking and taking action

1

## POW 1   PERSPECTIVE
*(knowing yourself and your audience)*

☐ Analyse yourself and your audience
to determine:

- ❑ Agreements, disagreements, and why
- ❑ Commonalities
- ❑ Culture (e.g. beliefs, behaviours, mores)
- ❑ Differences
- ❑ Environment
- ❑ Goals and objectives
- ❑ Knowledge, expertise and interest level
- ❑ Needs and desires
- ❑ Social, economic and educational background
- ❑ Viewpoints

2

## POW 2  PERCEPTION

*(how you perceive your audience and
how your audience perceives you)*

- ☐ Focus on ways to:
    - ❑ Build and sustain a positive relationship with your audience
    - ❑ Demonstrate expertise and knowledge
    - ❑ Exude self-confidence
    - ❑ Improve appearance
    - ❑ Keep an open mind
    - ❑ Maintain good poise
    - ❑ Understand cultural differences (e.g., beliefs, behaviours, mores)

3

## POW 3   PLANNING
*(determining the type and structure of
the presentation)*

☐   Answer the following questions:

    ❑   What will your topic be?

    ❑   When will your presentation
       ake place and for how long?

    ❑   Where will your presentation
       take place?

    ❑   Who will attend and how many?

    ❑   Why is your presentation
       being given?

4

### POW 3    PLANNING
*(determining the type and structure of the presentation)*

☐  Determine the strategy for
your presentation by deciding:

    ❏  What your audience wants

    ❏  What you want to accomplish

☐  Determine what tactics (e.g., actions)
to adopt to execute your strategy

☐  Determine the best time to give your
presentation

5

## POW 4    PREPARATION
*(developing the material)*

☐  Prepare an agenda that:

    ☐  Establishes where you are going

    ☐  Identifies what you plan to discuss

    ☐  Stands alone as a separate page

☐  Incorporate each of the fundamental components in your presentation:

    ☐  Logos (structure)

    ☐  Pathos (emotion)

    ☐  Ethos (credibility)

    ☐  What you want to accomplish

☐  Follow these guidelines to structure your presentation:

    ☐  Introduction – 10%

    ☐  Main body – 80%

    ☐  Conclusion – 10%

6

## *POW 4    PREPARATION*
### *(developing the material)*

☐   Select one or more logical structures:

- ☐   Introduction–Discussion–Conclusion
- ☐   Cause/effect
- ☐   Known/unknown
- ☐   Part/whole
- ☐   Problem(s)/solution(s)
- ☐   Questions/answers
- ☐   Simple/complex
- ☐   Time/Sequence
- ☐   Topical

7

## POW 4    PREPARATION
*(developing the material)*

☐ Prepare an introduction which has a:

    ☐ Purpose

    ☐ Scope

☐ Incorporate one or more of the following as an attention-getter in the introduction:

    ☐ Demonstration

    ☐ Question

    ☐ Quotation

    ☐ Startling statement

    ☐ Story

    ☐ Word

8

## POW 4   PREPARATION
*(developing the material)*

- ☐ Prepare the main body which:
    - ❑ Has a logical flow
    - ❑ Presents main ideas clearly
    - ❑ Unites main ideas with a single theme

- ☐ Incorporate one or more of the following into the main body:
    - ❑ Contrary views
    - ❑ Main ideas
    - ❑ Supporting facts, statistics, etc.

9

## POW 4    PREPARATION
*(developing the material)*

☐ Use one or more of the following
to support main ideas:
- ☐ Analogy
- ☐ Anecdotes
- ☐ Demonstrations
- ☐ Examples
- ☐ Exhibits/diagrams
- ☐ Expert opinions
- ☐ Facts
- ☐ Personal experiences
- ☐ Statistics
- ☐ Testimonials

10

## POW 4 PREPARATION
### (developing the material)

☐ Prepare a conclusion that:

    ☐ Calls for action

    ☐ Includes stories, quotes,
       illustrations, statistics, etc.

    ☐ Presents a summary of the main ideas

    ☐ Relates to the introduction

☐ Ensure that the pages of your presentation:

    ☐ Contain plenty of white space to break
       up the visual monotony

    ☐ Use some charts, diagrams, etc.
       for visual reinforcement and clarity

    ☐ Have lettering large enough for
       your audience to read

    ☐ Have no more than 9 items per
       page (7+2 rule)

    ☐ Present indented lists to
       show hierarchy

11

## POW 4    PREPARATION
*(developing the material)*

☐   Select the appropriate mode of delivery:

    ❏   Memory

    ❏   Narrative text

    ❏   Note cards

    ❏   Outline

12

## POW 4  PREPARATION
*(developing the material)*

☐   If relying on memory, be sure to memorize well

☐   If using narrative text, be sure to:

     ❑   Double/triple space for readability
     ❑   Keep handwriting/type large enough to read
     ❑   Not make their use obvious
     ❑   Not lose your place
     ❑   Use signposts in columns

13

## POW 4    PREPARATION
### (developing the material)

☐   If using note cards, be sure to:
- ❑   Avoid shuffling of cards
- ❑   Keep handwriting/type large enough to read
- ❑   Not make their use obvious
- ❑   Use a minimum of cards
- ❑   Use one note card per idea

☐   If using outlines, be sure to:
- ❑   Avoid shuffling of paper
- ❑   Double/triple space for readability
- ❑   Keep handwriting/type large enough to read
- ❑   Not make their use obvious
- ❑   Not lose your place
- ❑   Use signposts in columns

14

## POW 4 PREPARATION
*(developing the material)*

☐ Select type of visual aid to use:

- ☐ Audio tape
- ☐ Blackboard/whiteboard
- ☐ Flipchart
- ☐ Microcomputer/terminal
- ☐ Models
- ☐ Objects
- ☐ Overhead projector/slides
- ☐ Real objects
- ☐ Photographic slide projector
- ☐ Video disc
- ☐ Videotape

☐ Make sure visual aids are:

- ☐ Clean
- ☐ Clear
- ☐ Easy to use
- ☐ Manageable
- ☐ Relevant
- ☐ Understandable

15

## POW 4   PREPARATION
### (developing the material)

☐ Statistics should:
- ❑ Be kept to a minimum
- ❑ Be rounded numbers
- ❑ Support ideas

☐ Illustrations should:
- ❑ Be short and simple (KISS)
- ❑ Flow logically
- ❑ Show plenty of white space
- ❑ Be understandable
- ❑ Use colour sparingly

**16**

## POW 4    PREPARATION
### (developing the material)

☐   Check the environment to determine:
- ❑ Equipment
- ❑ Layout
- ❑ Lighting
- ❑ Noise level
- ❑ Seating capacity
- ❑ Size
- ❑ Sound system
- ❑ Spacing
- ❑ Supplies
- ❑ Temperature

17

## POW 5   PRACTICE
*(rehearsing to improve your performance)*

☐  Select the location for rehearsing:
- ❑  Actual location (preferred)
- ❑  Area similar to actual location

☐  Select ways to rehearse:
- ❑  In front of a mirror
- ❑  In front of friends/relatives/peers
- ❑  With a camcorder
- ❑  With a tape recorder

18

## POW 5 PRACTICE
*(rehearsing to improve your performance)*

- [ ] Follow these guidelines when rehearsing:
    - [ ] 'Vocalize' your presentation
    - [ ] Concentrate on appearance and how to present it, not the content
    - [ ] Rehearse as much as possible (minimum three times)
    - [ ] Recall as much as possible about your audience
    - [ ] Survey the presentation site
    - [ ] Prepare the rehearsal site to reflect the actual site

19

## POW 5   PRACTICE
*(rehearsing to improve your performance)*

☐ When rehearsing, strive to:
- ☐ Conquer stage fright
- ☐ Direct nervous energy into selected portions of your presentation
- ☐ Eliminate distracting mannerisms
- ☐ Practise body movement
- ☐ Synchronize physical actions with content
- ☐ Coordinate gestures with words
- ☐ Focus on the purpose
- ☐ Have a logical flow
- ☐ Learn the material
- ☐ Identify revisions to material and delivery
- ☐ Smooth out 'rough edges'
- ☐ Sound natural
- ☐ Speak clearly and loudly
- ☐ Use visual aids smoothly
- ☐ Improve timing
- ☐ Visualize the result
- ☐ Think positive

20

## POW 6 PERFORMANCE
*(delivering the presentation)*

☐ When standing in front of
an audience, be:

- ❏ Clear
- ❏ Confident
- ❏ Dynamic
- ❏ Enthusiastic
- ❏ Expressive
- ❏ Knowledgeable
- ❏ Natural
- ❏ Organized
- ❏ Pleasant
- ❏ Positive
- ❏ Precise
- ❏ Sensitive

21

## POW 6   PERFORMANCE
### (delivering the presentation)

☐   When delivering your presentation,
be sure to:

- ❏   Announce question and answer
ground rules
- ❏   Enunciate clearly
- ❏   Maintain eye contact with
your audience
- ❏   Maintain poise
- ❏   Move around the podium
- ❏   Pace yourself
- ❏   Project your voice
- ❏   Show an agenda
- ❏   Turn off the overhead projector
when not in use
- ❏   Use a pointer sparingly, e.g.
to show important features, words

22

## POW 6    PERFORMANCE
### (delivering the presentation)

☐   When delivering your presentation, avoid:

    ☐   Forgetting to add titles to
        each slide

    ☐   Making the print size of the slide
        difficult to read from far away

    ☐   Placing slides at an angle
        on the overhead projector

    ☐   Reading your slides

    ☐   Talking to your slides instead
        of your audience

    ☐   Using too many distracting words,
        e.g. 'ah' and 'you know'

    ☐   Saying offensive words related to
        religion, ethnicity, sexism or politics

    ☐   Using vulgarity and slang

    ☐   Walking back and forth in front
        of the projected image or slide

23

## POW 6   PERFORMANCE
*(delivering the presentation)*

☐ Recognize these potential sources
of communication problems:

- ❏ Body language
- ❏ Culture
- ❏ Language
- ❏ Mannerisms
- ❏ Listening skills
- ❏ Physical environment

24

261

## POW 6    PERFORMANCE
*(delivering the presentation)*

☐  Avoid these distracting mannerisms:

- ❏ Saying 'ahs', 'uhs', and 'you knows'
- ❏ Grasping pens/markers
- ❏ Placing hands in pockets
- ❏ Jingling coins in pockets
- ❏ Gripping/leaning on the podium
- ❏ Pacing back and forth
- ❏ Running fingers through your hair continuously
- ❏ Sneezing and coughing
- ❏ Waving the pointer

25

## POW 6    PERFORMANCE
*(delivering the presentation)*

☐ Combat stage fright by:

    ☐ Directing nervousness into body movement

    ☐ Directing nervousness into your pitch

    ☐ Ensuring plenty of rest the night before

    ☐ Learning as much as possible about your audience

    ☐ Mingling with your audience before speaking

    ☐ Recognizing that it's natural

    ☐ Taking a deep breath before speaking

    ☐ Thinking of your audience as friends

    ☐ Treating your audience as one person

26

## POW 6    PERFORMANCE
*(delivering the presentation)*

When delivering the introduction,

- ☐ Be sure to:
    - ☐ Be direct
    - ☐ Be relevant
    - ☐ Gesture positively
    - ☐ Maintain eye contact
    - ☐ Project confidence
    - ☐ Speak clearly
    - ☐ Start on time
    - ☐ Direct nervousness into your pitch

- ☐ Avoid:
    - ☐ Being pompous
    - ☐ Being insulting
    - ☐ Using sarcasm

27

## POW 6   PERFORMANCE
### (delivering the presentation)

When delivering the main body,

- ☐ Be sure to:
    - ❑ Be concise
    - ❑ Be understandable
    - ❑ Keep statistics to a minimum
    - ❑ Use good grammar

- ☐ Avoid:
    - ❑ Complex, multi-syllable words
    - ❑ Excessive adjectives and adverbs
    - ❑ Jargon
    - ❑ Trite phrases

28

## POW 6    PERFORMANCE
*(delivering the presentation)*

When delivering the conclusion,

- [ ] Be sure to:
    - [ ] Be direct
    - [ ] Be relevant
    - [ ] Use an attention-getter
    - [ ] Reinforce your credibility
    - [ ] Call for action
    - [ ] Leave the audience wanting more

- [ ] Avoid:
    - [ ] Speaking quickly just to get it over with
    - [ ] Using fine details

29

## POW 6   PERFORMANCE
*(delivering the presentation)*

☐   Select the best way(s) for handling questions:

    ❏   Allow other people to answer questions

    ❏   Repeat the question

    ❏   Rephrase the question

    ❏   Entertain written submission of questions

    ❏   Pause before answering a question

    ❏   If you don't know the answer, admit it

30

## POW 6    PERFORMANCE
*(delivering the presentation)*

☐ Consider the following regarding your voice:

    ❑ Articulation

    ❑ Pitch

    ❑ Rate/pace

    ❑ Volume

☐ When exercising effective listening skills:

    ❑ Maintain eye contact

    ❑ Use body language

    ❑ Paraphrase the speaker

    ❑ Ask for affirmation

    ❑ Use word signals

31

## POW 6    PERFORMANCE
### (delivering the presentation)

☐  Select ways to increase your audience's memory:

    ❑  Have a strong opening and closing

    ❑  Coordinate gestures with words or phrases

    ❑  Emphasize a word or phrase by lowering or raising pitch

    ❑  Emphasize key points through body movement and voice

    ❑  Employ metaphors, analogies and associations

    ❑  Use alliteration

    ❑  Employ repetition

    ❑  Beg the question

    ❑  Encourage active participation

    ❑  Take less time than allotted

**32**

## POW 6   PERFORMANCE
*(delivering the presentation)*

- ☐ If using humour, be sure it is:
  - ❑ Brief
  - ❑ Not overshadowing the main objective
  - ❑ Positive, not negative
  - ❑ Relevant
  - ❑ Inoffensive

33

## POW 6   PERFORMANCE
*(delivering the presentation)*

☐ If using visual aids, be sure to:
- ☐ Allow them to be seen by all members of your audience
- ☐ Leave them up only when relevant
- ☐ Not lean on them
- ☐ Present them in sequence
- ☐ Set them up before your presentation
- ☐ Talk to your audience, not the visual aid

☐ If using a flipchart, be sure to:
- ☐ Use print that is large enough and legible
- ☐ Use standard white paper
- ☐ Write keywords, not sentences
- ☐ Write on the front of every page, leaving the back blank

34

## POW 6    PERFORMANCE
*(delivering the presentation)*

☐ If using an overhead projector, be sure to:

    ❑ Connect to electrical outlet before making your presentation

    ❑ Position the machine so the image can be seen by all your audience

    ❑ Focus the projector being using

    ❑ Ensure a spare projector bulb is readily available

    ❑ Know how to replace a burnt-out bulb

    ❑ Keep marking pens handy

    ❑ Avoid blocking the image

    ❑ Never leave the platen blank and the machine running

    ❑ Never have the room pitch black

    ❑ Turn the machine off when not in use

35

## POW 6   PERFORMANCE
*(delivering the presentation)*

☐  When using slides, be sure to:
- ❏  Avoid clutter
- ❏  Employ colour to emphasize a point
- ❏  Give preference to pictures over words
- ❏  Have a background that is light and clean
- ❏  Keep to a minimum
- ❏  Never quote verbatim
- ❏  Leave showing only if relevant
- ❏  Pause before presenting and after removing from the projector

36

## POW 6    PERFORMANCE
*(delivering the presentation)*

☐   If using film, audio cassette, or videotape, be sure to:

    ☐   Explain purpose before showing

    ☐   Summarize after showing

    ☐   Use one monitor per 25 people

☐   If using music, consider:

    ☐   Determining the desired mood

    ☐   Playing it during breaks

    ☐   Using classical music, if possible

37

## POW 6    PERFORMANCE
*(delivering the presentation)*

☐   If distributing handouts, be sure to:
- ❏   Avoid reading them directly
- ❏   Have enough for everybody
- ❏   Be clear, concise and understandable
- ❏   Not conflict with your presentation
- ❏   Distribute after the presentation, if possible

38

## POW 6  PERFORMANCE
*(delivering the presentation)*

☐  To prevent 'turning off' an audience, avoid:

- ❑  Being arrogant
- ❑  Being pompous
- ❑  Using sarcasm
- ❑  Insulting/ridiculing listeners
- ❑  Using statistics and 'large' words
- ❑  Making excuses
- ❑  Reading text
- ❑  Telling personal problems

39

## POW 6  PERFORMANCE
*(delivering the presentation)*

☐  To prevent 'boring' an audience, avoid:
  ☐  Being unenthusiastic
  ☐  Hiding behind the podium
  ☐  Lack of eye contact
  ☐  No gesturing
  ☐  Reading from your slides
  ☐  Reading your presentation
  ☐  Talking in jargon
  ☐  Speaking in a monotone
  ☐  Using standards profusely
  ☐  Giving infrequent breaks
  ☐  Not involving your audience

40

## POW 6   PERFORMANCE
*(delivering the presentation)*

☐   To 'wake up' an audience, you can:

    ☐   Change a statement into a question

    ☐   Employ more body movement and vocal variety

    ☐   Encourage some physical or social interaction

    ☐   Give shorter, but more frequent breaks

    ☐   Present mental challenges

    ☐   Use demonstrations

    ☐   Walk into your audience

41